Dancing
with Raven
and Bear

Dancing
with Raven
and Bear

**A Book of Earth Medicine
and Animal Magic**

Sonja Grace

FINDHORN PRESS

Findhorn Press

One Park Street

Rochester, Vermont 05767

www.findhornpress.com

Findhorn Press is a division of Inner Traditions International

Disclaimer

The information in this book is given in good faith and intended for information only. Neither author nor publisher can be held liable by any person for any loss or damage whatsoever which may arise from the use of this book or any of the information therein.

A CIP record for this title is available from the Library of Congress

ISBN 978-1-62055-814-0 (print)
ISBN 978-1-62055-815-7 (ebook)

Printed and bound in Canada by Friesens Corporation.

10 9 8 7 6 5 4 3 2 1

Quote on pages 26–27: from *Towards an Archeology of the Soul* by Antero Alli © 2003

Edited by Michael Hawkins
Text design and layout by Damian Keenan
This book was typeset in Adobe Garamond Pro, Calluna Sans, with Pompeia Inline used as display typeface.

To send correspondence to the author of this book, mail a first-class letter to the author c/o Inner Traditions • Bear & Company, One Park Street, Rochester, VT 05767, and we will forward the communication, or contact the author directly at **https://sonjagrace.com**.

For Ian

ARTWORK BY SONJA GRACE

Contents

Introduction 9

1 Grounding 19

2 Dancing with Raven 25

3 Releasing Pain 29

4 Holding the Darkness at Bay 35

5 Power 41

6 Dreaming 49

7 The Burden 55

8 Death 61

9 The Illusion 67

10 A Safe Place 73

11 The Medicine Path 77

12 What Deer Had to Say… 85

13 Love 93

14 The River's Edge 101

15 Earth Spirit 109

16 Mending a Broken Heart 117

17 Warriors of the Earth 123

18 The Next Seven Generations 131

Conclusion 137

About the Author 143

'She traveled with Ravens and dreamed herself
into the mountain.'

Introduction

My name is Sonja Grace. I am a storyteller. I received these soul stories from my heart and they reflect my Norwegian and Native American heritage. My blood line includes Choctaw and Cherokee from my mother's side. Years ago, I was adopted on the Hopi Reservation and married into the tribe as well. Of all the blood lines coursing through my veins, I feel Hopi. I tease my Hopi family that I was captured by Vikings and stolen away from the tribe. I grew up in a Norwegian household and as a child, I remember hearing Norwegian folk-lore. The storieas often deapicted the great God Odin accompanied by two Ravens, named Huginn and Muninn. They were Odin's eyes and ears. They reported daily from the realm of Midgard, one of the nine worlds of Norse mythology. Huginn represents thought and Muninn is memory.

As I child I drew Ravens. I did not really understand why these birds were so prominent in my childhood artwork or why they had made their way so deeply into my psyche. It was only around 12 years old that I realized that these ancient beings had been speaking to me since I was a baby. As I approached young adulthood what they were saying actually started to make sense.

Now, they continue to not only speak to me but share incredible information from thousands of years ago. For example, in one of my recent *spirit travels* I met Odin and his son, Thor, the protector of mankind. Odin and Thor discussed with me the events of 12,000 years ago – the beginning of this phase of humanity.

In Norse history and legend, Odin's ravens are symbolic. The tale of Ragnar, an Old Norse King, tells of an embroidered banner he carried into battle bearing a raven called Reafan. The banner would flutter and move as the warriors headed into battle striking fear into the enemy because it invoked the power of Odin. Legend tells of the banner predicting the battle; if it did not move as the battle began then the battle was lost.

Ravens are also aligned with death and war because, like vultures and other birds of prey, they eat carrion. Other Norse myths suggest that the great God Odin and his ravens were linked together because Odin received fallen warriors at Valhalla. The ravens were considered manifestations of the Valkyries, the goddesses who selected the brave warriors as soldiers in Valhalla. Valkyries were known to shape-shift and would appear in the form of birds – most often ravens.

Of course, when the Vikings invaded England, Ireland and Wales they brought their mythic stories with them. The symbol of the raven and its power infiltrated the principalities and can be found throughout the United Kingdom including the Isle of Man. Superstition has it that if the ravens that live at the Tower of London should leave the Kingdom will fall.

Different Native American cultures view the Raven in a different light. The Raven can be a trickster or messenger. The indigenous people of the Pacific Northwest view the Raven as a magical creature with the ability to shape-shift into a human or animal. In Native American tradition the Raven is known for playing tricks, keeping secrets and allowing his greed to lead him down the path of gluttony. Even though the Raven is considered to be a trickster those hearing his stories often see him as a hero overcoming adversity.

The Lakota Sioux believe the Raven was once a white bird that warned the buffalo when a hunter was near. One day a shaman, angered by the Raven's warning to the buffalo, caught the Raven and threw him into the fire where he turned black. This is just one story; indigenous people have **many** stories of Raven.

In my stories, I experience Raven as a teacher and messenger. In my artwork whenever Raven is depicted sitting with a person they are always sitting on their head. It shows the connection of their spiritual center to Creator. The Raven brings messages and protects the crown of the head. Raven is that part of our psyche that chimes in and says I told you so!

In my Hopi tribe the Bear is believed to be the healer who grounds our energy and removes illness. Many indigenous people in America hold the same belief. Bear medicine is powerful and when used correctly it can heal. The Mount Shasta Indians tell the story of a girl raised by Grizzly Bears. She was no common girl, she was the daughter of the Chief of the Great Sky Spirits. He warned her never to stick her head out of the top of Mount Shasta because the wind would take her away from him and she would be gone.

She did not listen. One day she fell out of the top of Mount Shasta and was found by a mother Grizzly. The mother Grizzly raised the girl as her cub and years later allowed her to be married to her oldest Grizzly son. They brought unusual looking children into this world.

The mother Grizzly became old and knew she would soon die and felt she must come clean with the Chief of the Great Sky Spirits that she had his daughter. Once he learned where his daughter had been he came storming down the mountain. His footprints can be seen to this day on Mount Shasta, giant patches where nothing will grow. The Chief expected to see his little girl but instead a woman stood before him and strange creatures were gathered around her. He learned they were his grandchildren and with a rage of fury grabbed his daughter and took her back up the mountain. He cursed all grizzly bears, demanding they get on their hands and knees. He took away their ability to talk and made them walk on all fours. The strange grandchildren were cast out and wandered all over the Earth. According to Shasta legend they were the first Native American Indians.

Native American people love to tell stories in order to teach and to heal. Just like my ancestors I too am a storyteller. My personal experience of Raven and Bear comes from my heart and is woven with the influence of my heritage. My life as a mystic and healer has allowed me to be in service to Creator and the Earth. Daily I talk to people all over the world helping with broken hearts, the loss of a loved one and all kinds of health issues. I mend torn ligaments, blocked arteries and cancerous tumors throughout the body. I see where the client is resistant and how tricky their ego has become to shield them from their truth. Much of my healing ability comes from the many indigenous stories that I embody. Earth Medicine connects us to the truth. To me the stories in *Dancing with Raven and Bear* remind us that the simplicity of the Earth and all that we have been given can get lost in a complicated technological world. The answers are often in the stories. It is through the Earth and her energy that we are able to connect and learn what real freedom is.

Animals provide different forms of healing. A beloved dog or cat sitting on your lap soothes and calms while a wild animal crossing our path can provide a sign. There are many helpers in the animal kingdom and though we may not be aware of it, there is *animal magic*. Each person has an animal related to the chakra (energy center). The animal totem is seven in total and brings forth a voice from each energy center allowing us to connect and listen to the wild with new eyes and ears.

We all travel with our animal helpers, guides and angels and our dreams take us to places we long to be. My dreams have always been a mix of my current life, the past as well as the future. In my work I use two concepts of dreaming. The first is the one we experience while we sleep and the second is a form of dreaming that takes place in meditation. We can dream ourselves into the mountain if we so choose by sitting in meditation. We can dream ourselves into a better world, one that connects us to Earth Medicine or a natural relationship with the Earth.

What motivates us at a deeper level is the pursuit of a spiritual connection. Many people find themselves on a spiritual quest but while they are searching for their connection to source they often bypass the powerful natural elements around them. The truth of this is represented in one of my drawings in Chapter 2 called, *Dancing with Raven* which depicts a woman who is hungry and talkative and never satisfied. This is often experienced in our spiritual quest. There is a gathering of information which is endless but a lack of true connectivity through real and actual spiritual practice. The Raven in the picture represents how we are inundated with information about the 'spiritual movement' and like many other things bright and shiny we grasp for it without any actual experience or understanding of the spirit realm and what it offers. We think we deserve to know everything, but I believe that there are some things in the world that we are not meant to be the keepers of. Some medicine is far more powerful than what most people can handle. Which is why this kind of 'healing' ability is possessed by only a few. The greatest connection between all things that are bright and shiny and the Raven's desire to possess those things is our ego.

The misuse of energy and magic is common, especially when the inner work has not been addressed. For example, an individual may feel that they want to help humanity but, they have not yet healed their own wounded inner child. I call this the trend of 'The Wounded Healer' in which many people rush for spiritual power and knowledge but are often unable to handle it once they get it. From my perspective, it is important to approach all spiritual matters with respect and honor. The Raven and the Bear teach us to be responsible for our actions and possess spiritual accountability.

At the center of my spiritual stories the reader will find the tension between light and darkness. In Chapter 4 the story is about holding darkness at bay. It discusses how we have been teaching through dualism since the beginning of time. The Bear represents the inner part of us that has faith. We find this mythical creature singing songs to bring in the light and thus teaching us that by using our genuine voice and speaking our truth we can hold darkness at bay. The Bear shows us how to bring sound and light together. Our relationship to the Earth is the fundamental reason we humans are here. It is a relationship that needs to be rekindled and better understood.

Also, in this chapter, I reveal some ways in which we can use medicinal plants to help us manage the negative energies in today's world. Cedar, sage, sweet-grass and other natural plant life, provide healing, clearing and blessings. These plant medicines have been used for centuries by Native Americans and indigenous people around the world to cure and remove unwanted energies. We feel the darkness but do not always have the tools to hold it at bay or completely clear the energy.

Of course, one of the biggest fears we all have is of death. Through folklore, myths and legends people around the world have explored the fear of death but over time these stories have been forgotten. We no longer embrace death and understand it is a rite of passage to the next world. Instead we spend money, time, energy, pain and sorrow trying to avoid what we will all ultimately face. It is the most powerful passage, aside, from birth, that we will experience. In *Dancing with Raven and Bear* I hope to teach through their stories how we can better embrace the final transformation to the other side. I work with people and their past lives and I am able to reveal the many varied lives they have lived, as well as the many deaths that they have experienced. Our cultural experiences are as varied as our perceptions of death and dying. I have found that through Earth Medicine we can remember who we truly are and that we are as transient as the leaves that fall from the trees to cover the ground in the fall.

Chapter Nine is called *The Illusion* and the story is about a woman hiding in the mountains who wants to have a new life because she does not like the one she is living. The story is all about illusion and it reflects something that I have discovered in my many years of counseling others – most people are heavily invested in the illusion. In many cases the illusion can take the form of addictions such as shopping, alcohol, drugs, social media, food and so forth. We create the illusion by believing more in the dogma or belief systems of society rather than looking at the energy of what we are manifesting. When we discover what the illusion is and own up to our creation of it then we can better connect with the true magic of the Earth.

For me, magic is the unseen energy that connects us deeply to our core. The story asks us how many times we have tried to disguise ourselves hoping no one would notice us? The responsibility lies with each of us to choose to either keep our eyes open and face the illusion or to choose to continue to hide.

My Hopi family would say that what we teach our children goes on to effect the next *seven* generations. Children born today are often more highly sensitive than their predecessors and need direction. By teaching our children the ways of Earth Medicine they will learn how to identify and manage *energy*. In my view, many of today's children are *star seeds* who will help to usher in a new phase of humanity. These children are so highly developed that they come forth with a warrior stance to protect the Earth. Not only do children feel this urgency to protect our planet, it is becoming clear that many people today have felt a calling to help the Earth and their fellow human beings – there is a slow awakening taking place. I described these events in my book *Become an Earth Angel*. The survival of our species is in the hands of future generations, which is why teaching the simple truths of Earth Medicine is a very powerful and vital tool. Each one of these stories contains a healing element – a deeper truth that can touch our daily lives.

Earth Medicine can also be described as medicine for the soul. It is a way to take care of ourselves naturally. I believe that our souls are infinite and while we think that we understand this one human experience we are living – we really do not. Actually, our incarnation into physical form is accompanied by a state of amnesia – we forget our soul journey. Consequently, we block the information we carry at a soul level and create an environment where our karma must play out and ultimately heal. We spend lifetimes looking for a connection to Source that would heal the core wound of separation and this is the main impetus behind humanity's desire for a sense of unity. In other words, the very thing (separation) that we wrestle with on a daily basis is the meaning (unity) of our lives.

The stories in *Dancing with Raven and Bear* have been given to me to help all of us navigate how to take care of ourselves, emotionally, mentally, spiritually and physically while living on Earth. Lest we forget, the Earth works in unity with herself, she is a warehouse of knowledge for all that live upon her. All life has a natural connection with Earth. Everything is in place for us to take care of ourselves. What we need is the awareness to embrace our true nature while living on this planet.

'She sat with her ravens contemplating
her next move. She was grounded.
She was content. She was free.'

1

Grounding

There was a girl who sat in meditation for so long her hair grew into a Raven. Her mind released all that she was attached to and she began to feel peaceful. As she let things go her body relaxed and the Raven on her head called out to his friends. They sat in her lap and had a noisy talk. They discussed the weather and the latest news. It was so loud she felt the noise dissolve into nothing. She could feel her body was no more. The birds were weightless in her arms. Her energy started to dissolve and merge with the Ravens and the air around her—joining with all that was. The Ravens grew quiet and whispered in her ear. "Be free little one. Allow yourself to be free." She felt a deep peace that was indescribable and encompassed all that she was and all that she knew. She felt wings sprout out of her back and her body changed; feathers emerged, and a large beak formed where her mouth was. She took flight with the other birds and realized her human form was not who she really was.

Everything is made up of energy. We have an electromagnetic field around our body that is charged by the Earth's energy and keeps that big space around us called the aura in place. Living in the fifth dimension requires us to ground our energy deep into the Earth.

> *"The fifth dimension is the same vibration as the fifth chakra, with a high frequency and connectivity through the electromagnetic field among all living things. The color frequency is indigo, with a sound tone of E flat, which makes us increasingly telepathic and acutely aware of the space between this world and the spirit universe."*
>
> — SONJA GRACE, *Become an Earth Angel*

Grounding allows the nature of our existence to be assisted by the planet. The Earth's energy is a strong vibrational force that informs us on all levels. When we feel out of sorts it is time to ground. Bringing Earth energy up into your body is as important as grounding your energy into the planet. Our bodies are like conduits receiving energy from the Divine above and Earth energy up through our feet. The two energy forces meet at the heart. It is here that creativity and manifestation take place.

Here is a simple exercise for being a conduit.

Medicine Tree Pose

Go outside and stand next to a tree. Feel the Earth's energy rise up through your feet and fill your body. At the same time, feel the divine flowing through the top of your head. Allow the marriage of Earth and Sky to take place in your heart. With your eyes closed begin to feel that you are having the same experience as the tree.

You might want to express that synergy of fusion with this following prayer.

Earth Medicine Prayer

Thank you, Mother Earth, for the air I breathe, the ground I walk on, the food grown in your soil and the seasons that show me the cycle of life. I recognize these are your gifts and I am grateful. My heart is filled with love as I send rays of love to my inner core; I also send rays of love deep down into the ground, filling you Mother Earth, with my gratitude. May I create peace upon your land and care for you the way I care for my children and loved ones. May I walk softly so that I might hear your song and celebrate in your beauty each and every day.

Earth Medicine Grounding Meditation

Close your eyes and allow your breathing to slow, as you take air in through your nose and out through your nose, with the tongue resting gently on the roof of the mouth. If this is uncomfortable, then breathe in whatever way is best for you.

Drop your consciousness into the first chakra and feel the floor or chair beneath you. Create a cone of energy from the first chakra, with the smaller opening of the cone at the chakra and the wide base going all the way down to the center of the Earth. Never send your chakra anywhere; you are simply creating a cone of energy that goes all the way down to the center of the Earth in order to ground it.

Now go into your belly, the second chakra, and create a cone of energy that goes over the first cone all the way down, deeper and deeper, to the center of the Earth, and ground it.

Feel your consciousness in your solar plexus, or the third chakra, and imagine it like a clear, calm lake. Create a third cone of energy that goes over the first two cones, watching it go down, deeper and deeper, further and further, to the center of the Earth, and ground it. Feel the tremendous base you have with the first three chakras grounded!

Now go into your heart, or fourth chakra, and let it be like a three-dimensional sun with rays of love shining out toward others and rays of love shining in toward you. Create a cone of energy from the fourth chakra and see it going down inside the first three cones, all the way to the center of the Earth.

Take your consciousness into your fifth chakra and feel your throat, soft and supple. Create a cone of energy, and feel it traveling down inside the heart cone, deeper and deeper, further and further, to the center of the Earth, and ground it.

Go into your sixth chakra, or forehead, and let your mind be clear, as if you are looking at a blank movie screen. Create a cone of energy that goes inside the other cones, letting it travel deeper and deeper, further and further, to the center of the Earth, and ground it.

Move into the seventh chakra or the top of your head, and allow it to open like a flower, blossoming open. Create a cone of energy that goes inside all the other cones and ground it deep into the Earth.

Acknowledge your higher self and God and the Goddess. Ask that everything you do be in accordance with the will of God for the highest good of everyone and the highest good of the universe.

Ask for the violet flame to transmute any negative energy, any negative thought forms, up into light and love. Ask Source for the white light, the golden light, and the blue light to descend and fill every cell in your body.

"This grounding meditation allows you to ground your energy, as well as receive energy from the Earth. The Earth's energy charges our energy systems throughout the physical body. When we use this grounding meditation, we can connect cones of energy deep into the Earth and align with the Divine. When our energy is grounded, we are able to help others and recognize we do not have to engage our energy into the situation to be helpful."

— SONJA GRACE, *Become an Earth Angel*

Once you have grounded yourself and feel connected to the Earth you should start to notice how you feel, and sense where in your physical body you are holding energy or resisting and creating tension. Use your breath when grounding so you can address any areas of resistance. Sit quietly and contemplate your next move.

'There was a dance she did with Raven.
It brought her joy as she flew through the air
feeling the wind on her face.
She was like the bird, talkative and hungry.'

2

Dancing with Raven

There was a woman who loved to dance. She would dance so hard she would try to defy gravity and float up into the air laughing and talking with Raven. She told Raven she had wanted to be a bird her whole life. She danced and danced making movements like she was trying to grow wings and fly. One day she had an idea to ask Raven for help. Raven agreed and gave her some magic. Then, she started growing wings and sprouting feathers and in one big whoosh she was flying!

Together the woman and Raven danced together in the sky. Raven was delighted he had a friend, but she didn't have the understanding or the navigation to manage the wings of a bird. Suddenly, she came crashing to the ground unable to move, both of her wings were broken. She was devastated. She had failed at her one chance to be a bird and fly. Raven came to her and told her that next time she must learn how to navigate before she asked for such power and magic. He said that she must understand the gravity and importance of carrying this kind of medicine.

She felt the ground beneath her and could smell cedar all around her. The wings and feathers were gone. The woman got up and asked the cedar tree for permission to use the tree's medicine. The cedar tree granted her permission and she picked some of the greens. She burned the cedar and used the smoke to clear herself and make amends to Creator. She humbled herself. Afterwards, her dancing changed, and she moved with intention, understanding the gravity of her energy and the Earth.

In Norse myth and Native American folklore, the Raven is a powerful bird. It is often described as the messenger or magician who can mimic the sounds of humans and other animals. In centuries past, Ravens literally carried messages from one kingdom to another. In the stories of Odin, the Raven God in Norwegian folklore, they were believed to be messengers between worlds. Ravens are also associated with war and death. Many of the Norse stories about Odin and Thor tell of Huginn and Muninn, who are the two mythical Ravens that accompany Odin. The tales warn us of the power of Raven medicine; if used for good it can create an opening to other realms but if it is misused then it will backfire. The stories teach us that we must respect this bird and all winged ones.

Ravens are also portrayed as shape-shifters, especially in the ancient stories that originate from the Pacific Northwest region of North America and as far away as the far Northern European Nordic countries. In their folklore, some characters have the ability to transform into a Raven and either bring goodness and healing or they might be portrayed as the trickster who delivers difficult teachings. Native American, tribal people have understood the magic and power of the Raven for centuries.

"Though ravens and crows are often confused for the same bird, they exhibit many differences. Ravens are always

larger than crows and possess a far greater vocabulary for communicating with each other. Where crows act skittish on the ground and flap frenetic in flight, ravens exhibit calm confidence on land and soar the skies much like hawks, condors, and eagles.

Ravens live far away from people in the forests and mountains; crows flock in and around every major city. If you live in a city, most likely you have only seen crows. The raven also appears in many mythologies of the world's cultures. In Celtic lore, "The Morrighan" is the Raven Goddess of Fate, Battle and Sovereignty (also called "The Great Queen"), who determines whether or not a warrior walks off the field of battle or is carried off upon his shield. Pacific Northwest indigenous tribes (Haida, Tlingit, Tsimshian, Kwakiutl, Nisgaa-Gitksan, and Salishan), see the Raven as a trickster archetype who helps people as a complex heroic figure with negative and positive traits. In ancient Greek mythology, ravens were linked with Apollo, the god of prophecy, and acted as the god's messengers in the mortal world."

— ANTERO ALLI, *Towards an Archeology of the Soul*

As I have already noted, there are often great consequences to misusing the Raven's extremely powerful medicine. For example, in many of the stories we learn how those who engage in sorcery often find themselves dealing with much more than they bargained for. This is particularly true for those who are not aware of or have not looked at their own dark side. Repeatedly we see how vital it is that we recognize where we are wounded and need healing before we attempt any kind of energy medicine.

Raven is a constant reminder to stay within our abilities and what we have prepared for. The Raven misses nothing;

always flying high above events or sitting up high on a branch or tree to gain perspective of all things.

Symbolically, the feathers of the Raven are the color of the night sky and represent the vast pathway to Source. Ravens are also associated with healing – the Raven is the character who mimics and scavenges bringing the essential medicine to the table. Raven loves ceremony and attends with the intent to carry healing to those in need. When the Raven appears, it offers the opportunity to go beyond what you know or what you think might have happened because the magic of Raven allows us to experience something far beyond our earthly understanding.

Dancing with Raven is about allowing ourselves to experience the alchemy of *Earth Medicine* or in other words the magic that lives in all nature. Or are we like the woman in the story, who becomes talkative and hungry, and eager for more power? In my experience someone who meditates regularly and connects deeply with the Earth will be ready to ask Raven for the proper teachings. Respect, integrity and love will guide you to work from a much higher place.

3

Releasing Pain

Her heart was filled with sorrow. She had died and was stuck between worlds. Raven saw her in the forest unable to move from where she stood. Raven shifted into the realm that had her between worlds. He said, "Follow me!" She knew Raven would take her to Bear. Her heart was heavy, and she feared she would never reach the light. She told Bear that she had died suddenly, leaving her children and husband behind. She was not ready to go and could not accept such a passage had taken place.
Bear said tenderly, "You must give your pain to the Earth," and he led her to the mountain.

When they arrived at the foot of the snow-capped ridge a giant doorway opened up in the mountain and Raven beckoned her to enter. She stepped inside with Bear. Standing in the center of the cave, in an ancient medicine wheel, was a magnificent being who she knew to be the Goddess of the Earth. The Goddess held out her arms to embrace her. She felt the warmth and safety of the Earth and thanked her. Then the woman reached into her pocket and found some sacred tobacco. She gave an offering to the Goddess and dropped to her knees, overwhelmed with gratitude.

The Goddess placed her hands on the woman's head and as she did so, she let out a primal sound that went deep into the Earth. As the Goddess turned her to face each direction within the medicine wheel, she convulsed, and all of her pain come rushing out of her body. The Goddess smiled, "Let it go, your children will survive, and your husband will overcome his sorrow. It is time for you to go to Creator and no longer suffer."

*'Bear held her in his arms while her sorrow
filled the mountains.'*

Tears streamed down the woman's face. She looked up at the Goddess and said, "How can I go with my children growing up, playing in the forest, without me..." Her voice trailed off and tears flooded down her cheeks.

The Goddess replied, "You are directly connected to your ancestors who taught you to call upon them for their help. You will grieve, and it will take time, but you must not take this loss into your own being. Ground your energy deep into my soil and keep releasing your pain. The cycle of life on Earth is short and karma can bring great suffering." She looked into the woman's eyes and said, "Now you must heal from this terrible loss."

Raven brought her the moon and held it up so that she could see her reflection. At first, she saw a haggard woman whose dark circles under her eyes gave her a ghoulish look. Raven cackled, "Look again!" She looked once more at the moon and a beautiful Eagle was looking back at her. She smiled noticing her eagle beak didn't turn up at the corners of her mouth. The Goddess replied, "Your ability to shape-shift into an eagle will help you to make your journey home." The woman shook her feathers and stood tall.

The Goddess embraced her and bid her to go into the forest and feel her body, mind and spirit as one. "Allow nature to heal you from this tragic loss as you make your way to Creator."

The Eagle nodded and looked at Bear who was waiting for her by the entrance to the mountain. She flew out and the large doorway closed after them. The Eagle looked back and was filled with gratitude to have had such a meeting with the Goddess. She swooped down to Bear and thanked him. Then she playfully chased Raven overhead. Her wings picked up the wind that took her up past the trees tops.

Bear and Raven looked up and could see her circling way above the forest.

She continued to rise until they could no longer see her.

Sudden death is extremely difficult for both the deceased and the family members left behind. The bereaved are never ready for such a tragic experience. What we don't realize however, is that sudden death is often a shock to the deceased who at times can get caught between worlds. They are not ready to accept what has befallen them. They are as confused and surprised as their loved ones because they were just alive and there was no expectation of their death. Sometimes, family members are so astonished at their loved one's death that the deceased literally avoids going to the light. Their intention to help their family members without having first gone to the spirit realm jeopardizes their ultimate safe passage to the other side – this is why we have ghosts.

When Raven sees the woman stuck between worlds he realizes what has happened because she is in spirit form. In his own medicine he knows how to access the realms. Bear who is the medicine man takes her to the mountain where his father took him to meet the Goddess.

The Goddess of the Earth makes sure the woman's sorrow is released in all four directions. She does this because each direction contains a different energy, purpose and understanding which helps the deceased to be released from Earth. The living constantly walk the medicine wheel – it represents the circle of life, the four directions, above and below. We begin in the south with the color red and the gate all people travel through when they die, across the Milky Way. All life comes from this direction. In the west we find introspection and the color black. It is in the west that we look within ourselves and communicate with the inner child. The north is associated with the color white and a place of wisdom. We are challenged in the north through endurance, hardship and ultimately cleansing. Yellow is the color of the east, where we greet the sun. The early morning rays of light help us to see what is true. This direction is a place where all things are illuminated. We find Creator above and the color blue and the Goddess or Earth below in the color green. These well-traveled roads are what we connect with daily. Once the woman has released her emotional pain, she understands from her journey around the medicine wheel that her family is going to be OK. She transforms into an eagle and ascends to Creator.

I lived in New York City after 9/11. There are many energies to contend with in the city but when I would walk near the World Trade Center site I would find myself crying uncontrollably. I was able to see all the people who were stuck between worlds, not only the victims of the tragedy but the first responders as well. I spent months helping people to the light. Since then I have worked with a client who rebuilt the World Trade Center site, now called The Freedom Tower. He came across ghosts and spirits that needed assistance. To this day, I help many spirits who are stuck between worlds. There are rare occasions when they are truly meant to be here and serve a purpose such as those drowned sailors who linger near rocks to warn ships passing by.

Our understanding of ghosts is pretty much left to individual experiences and folklore. The ghosts of dead people in Norse mythology are called Draugar. These ghosts are not content and leave their burial mounds to harass the living often causing insanity, illness and even death. The people believed if a person died, having committed crimes, they would often come back as ghosts and wreak havoc on the locals. Buried bodies would be moved to new grave sites in hopes that the dead would rest in peace.

The woman's transformation into an eagle represents a state of spiritual peace. The eagle is an important part of Native culture. Eagles represent a magical element that spiritually oversees most ceremonies. My own understanding of this medicine is that eagle takes our prayers to Creator.

4

Holding the Darkness at Bay

Creator came to Bear one day and gave him a drum. He told Bear that he must sing his songs when there is darkness he cannot escape. Bear took this very seriously and practiced every day. The Earth heard him singing and taught him songs for the water and the rain. He would go to the river and sing to the water, his tears running down his face… his love ran deep for the Earth.

One day, Bear noticed a darkness coming towards him. This cloud grew bigger and bigger and Bear started to sing. He sang his songs and beat his drum so loud he was sure Creator would hear him. He called out to Creator but did not get an answer. He worried Creator could not see or hear him because the darkness was becoming so strong. The Earth's energy came up through his feet and Bear suddenly felt grounded and not afraid. He heard the Goddess whisper, "You must use your light with each song." Bear was confused. "What is my light and how can I find anything with such darkness around me?" he asked himself.

The Earth's energy rose up into his legs right past his belly and into his heart. Suddenly a bright light came streaming out of bear's chest and Bear started to sing and dance and play his drum. His voice was clear, and the sound waves mixed with the light waves beaming from his heart. As Bear sang his song the darkness began to shrink down into nothing and very soon it was gone as quickly as it arrived. Creator stood in front of Bear and said, "I am happy you have found the answer to the darkness.

'There were many songs Bear sang to bring
in the light. He held the darkness at bay.'

I have always been with you. My energy flows through the top of your head down to your heart and meets the Earth's energy fusing together to create light. This light, combined with your voice, is like a tapestry woven together as a protection from all evil."

He smiled at Bear and said, *"You will always hold the darkness at bay."*

There are many ways Earth Medicine can help us to heal and clear the darkness away. Before we begin to use the natural gifts the Earth provides, we must respect and understand that each living thing has a spirit. One way to show reverence for all living things is to ask permission before picking or cutting a plant, taking a rock or anything from nature.

In Native American cultures tobacco is used as an offering. I always carry a little tobacco and use it to pray with before gathering cedar or any of the other plants I use as a part of my practice. If you do not have tobacco to give, perhaps you can place a small amount of food for the spirit of the plant or rock. It is my belief that we must feed these unseen elements – just as we would feed our own family. We do not have to put a whole table of food out (although there are cultures who do this), just a tiny amount to make an offering.

In my opinion, the Western or Pacific Red Cedar tree is the best plant to use when clearing negative energy. First, I make an offering to the tree. Then I feel that I have permission to pick the greens from the tree and hang them up to dry. Once the greens are dry, I like to burn a small amount in a fire-safe bowl or coffee can. When I light this, I allow it to flare up first and then I blow the fire out. I use the smoke throughout the house and body. This is called smudging. This clears out negative energies. **Cedar** smudge sticks are also great to use but it is important to obtain a fire-safe bowl or coffee can as that will prevent any stray pieces from falling away. You can use Juniper in the same way as it is related through Earth Medicine to the Cedar tree.

I use **Sage** for blessings. You can pick sage in the desert or grow sage in your garden. Remember to give an offering to the plant before you harvest. The smoke used from dried sage leaves is a way of asking Creator to bless an object, baby, house or ceremony. Sage has been mistaken by some people as the plant medicine to be used to clear away negative energy. Unfortunately, that has the wrong effect and actually blesses the negativity. Sage is a very sacred plant and needs to be honored for the Earth Medicine it holds.

Sweet Grass is used by many tribes in ceremony. This plant is considered the oldest plant on earth by the Ojibwe and Cree, who refer to it as the hair of Mother Earth. During sacred times the long grass is braided into bundles. The spirit of this plant is one that has assisted and protected many ceremonies.

Our four-legged friends, the winged ones, trees, plants and humans take their physical or dense form from the Earth. The Earth herself holds vast amounts of energy that is expressed in all forms of life. However, the soul of those life forms, be it a tree, animal or human has incarnated from somewhere else in the universe.

We are all made up of organic material and so by connecting our energy with the Earth's energy we create a powerful way to receive what we need when confronted by dark forces.

Dark forces are a part of dualism; the good and bad, right and wrong, light and dark. If we allow ourselves to dive into our fear, we are investing in the illusion of the duality. In order to protect ourselves we can connect by grounding our energy deep into the Earth. By going further in meditation, we will find inner peace and better observe the duality. Deep meditation allows us to step back as an observer and no longer engage any part of our energy into whatever is negatively confronting us. When our fear is activated by dark forces we give them power over us but if we chose instead to only observe, that power is diminished. In a state of observation, we connect with a much higher frequency that is source.

'*Bear knew Raven was still trying to protect him.*'

5

Power

Being a medicine-man, Bear understood the responsibility he had to not misuse his powers. He helped the other bears and animals of the forest and occasionally humans. One day while he was gathering herbs for a wound on a fox's leg, he saw Raven talking to the wind. Bear yelled, "What are you doing Raven?" Raven responded, "I told the wind we need to clear the surrounding land around this forest of all humans."

Raven was having a particularly hard day. He lost one of his brothers to a human's mistake.

Bear looked at Raven. "What are you talking about?" he asked.

"Humans are getting closer and closer to our home. We need to protect our kind," he answered bitterly.

Bear asked, "What do you know about asking the wind for such things?"

"I heard other Ravens talking about how the wind can change the entire landscape," he replied. "I thought that sounded good."

Bear put down his herbs. He walked towards where Raven was sitting on a low branch in a cedar tree.

"What makes you think the wind won't take away our homes?"

Raven cocked his head to one side, "I never thought of that."

The gentle breeze that was floating through the forest started to build and become stronger. Leaves and pine needles stirred on the forest floor.

Raven cawed, "It looks like the wind heard me! Time to go." Squawking, he flew off into the woods.

Bear yelled after him, "You don't know what you have done."

Bear quickly gathered his herbs and called to the forest community. Deer, rabbit, fox, elk, mice, porcupine, squirrel, eagle, hawk, skunk and other bears all arrived. He told them, "Raven has called upon the wind to wipe out any humans getting closer to our home. He doesn't know what he has done. I must go and undo this. For the time being I urge you all to take cover and hide in the caves. You will be safe there."

Now, the wind began to howl. Bear grabbed his medicine bag and took off at an urgent pace. He arrived at the center of the forest where a large tree loomed overhead. He stood on his back legs and spoke in his native tongue to the tree. "May I have entrance?" "Yes," replied the tree and the bark split apart like two large doors opening.

Bear entered the tree and immediately started descending an ancient set of stone stairs. At the bottom was another door. Bear began to utter words from the ageless dialect that only bears spoke. The door opened, and he entered a vast cave beneath the Earth. He went to the center of it. Bear knew that the wind lived here between the two rocks deep inside the cave. Bowing before the rocks he addressed the wind in a formal fashion. Suddenly, a fierce woman appeared, strong and powerful. Bear knelt before her. "Please understand that I come in peace and respect for all that you do for the planet. I ask that you reconsider what Raven has requested," he said.

"Why?" asked the wind.

Shocked by her directness, Bear stammered his answer.

"There is a natural balance that must exist between the wild and the human population," Bear told her. "To cleanse the forest of all humans could also mean the removal of those

who respect us," he explained. Bear took a step closer to the wind and in a soft voice said, "I do not want to disrespect you. I humbly ask that you reconsider what Raven has asked for and understand his recent loss has lead him to seek revenge."

The woman shimmered as waves of light passed through her. "I will consider this," she said thoughtfully. "But I need time to make my final decision."

Bear thanked her for this sacred meeting and left a medicine offering. He turned towards what he thought was the direction of the doorway. But instead of the door he could see a woman leaning over a pool of water further into the cave. Bear walked towards her.

"Who are you?"

"I am the keeper of all that is sacred in this cave. I tend to the elements of wind, fire and water keeping them safe," she said.

Bear lowered his head, "It is an honor to meet you."

Bear understood the energies of these ancient sites. He knew the magic was strong and before long he felt its power begin to overwhelm him. He struggled to keep his eyes open and chose to rest by the water. Finally giving in to the energy of this ancient place Bear lost consciousness and fell into a deep sleep.

He dreamed of the forest being devoured by wind and fire. He saw his parents running for their lives and the humans running with water trying to put out the flames. Bear watched as his family and friends were unable to outrun the smoke and intense heat – everything melting away as the flames ravaged the land. He woke with tears streaming down his face. The priestess was next to him.

"Why must I have such a nightmare?" he asked.

Reaching out, she wiped his brow. "You needed to see what kind of power these elements have."

Bear shook his head, "I have seen such destruction before."

She whispered, "The wind is anxious to keep the land cleared of all unwanted energies. Fire will always stand by her for they are after the same thing – purification. It is a natural phenomenon on Earth."

Bear looked off in the distance and said, "But there are humans who do not disturb our home and walk through the woods with reverence and respect."

"That is true. But there are also humans who would be careless with the element of fire and allow it to destroy our home. The relationship between fire, wind and water is sacred to the Earth. The Earth knows that they all play a part in protecting her. She also knows the relationship between these elements must be kept in balance the same way you described the balance between the forest and the humans. Your dream is about the carelessness of humans with all that is sacred," she remarked.

"But Raven was upset when he asked the wind to cleanse the land, he didn't know what he was saying. The humans have not harmed the forest for a long time."

The woman smiled and told Bear that she admired his belief in humans. As a high priestess from a time long forgotten she has seen many catastrophic events take place on Earth and so she remained here as a guardian.

"What do you suggest I do?" asked Bear.

"I think you have done what you came to do; to stop the wind and allow Raven to see his revenge is misleading him."

Bear was sitting with his back against the wall of the cave, a small fire was flickering on the other side of the large cavern. Bear stood and walked toward it, his anger rising as he approached the sacred flame.

The priestess moved toward him. "Let your anger go," she said. "Let it be dissolved in the fire."

"I can't, I won't let it go, this fire killed my parents!" he cried out.

The priestess put her hand in the middle of Bear's back and gently stated what Bear knew to be the truth. "They had to go so you could become who you are today."

Tears spilled onto his cheeks. He stared into the flame and watched with wonder as his parents suddenly appeared to him and spoke to him lovingly, "We are sorry we had to leave you when you were so young. We never meant to hurt you. We wanted you to be strong and become the medicine-man we always knew you would be. We sacrificed our own lives for yours."

Then he witnessed something extraordinary. Something he had never known until this moment. There in the fire he saw himself, running, running with all the other bears away from the burning heat – and then as the flames licked at his paws Raven swooped from above and lifted the little Bear into the sky to a safe location. At once it was clear, Raven was still trying to protect him.

Bear gazed up at the priestess. She was smiling. He reached into his medicine bag and once again made an offering to the fire. He asked the fire to forgive him. He now understood why his parents were taken. Bear asked the fire to respect his home and stay out of the forest.

"I only come when there is a need for cleansing," said the fire. "My medicine is for the Earth. All who live upon her must respect these elements."

Bear nodded. He turned to the priestess, "I am ready to go home."

Now the door opened, and Bear made his way up the long staircase that wound up the tree trunk. Once at the top he spoke the ancient words that released him from the tree. He stepped out into the forest.

The wind was strong as he made his way back to his camp. Raven was waiting for him. Bear put down his medicine bag and walked up to Raven. He put his arms around Raven and hugged him.

Raven squawked, "What is this for?"

With tears welling in his eyes Bear told Raven his story and how he had seen in the fire what Raven had done for him. Bear explained that now he understood why Raven had asked the wind to help him. Bear also told Raven that he had learned that it is important not to ask these elements for help—unless you could be sure that you are clear of any anger, resentment or fear.

"They are very powerful," said Bear "and there are consequences to misusing these energies."

Raven nodded. He told Bear that ever since the fire he had always been in his watchful eye. He would try to protect the forest for as long as he lived.

Bear smiled, "Do not worry, Raven, I have spoken to the priestess who cares for the fire, water and wind. She assured me the natural order will keep us safe."

Raven cackled. The winds died, and the trees shimmered in the early morning light.

For centuries humans have warred and fought with each other for power. Humans want power for a variety of reasons: to be in charge, to rule, to have the final say over the fate of families, communities, countries or the world. Humans crave power like they crave food.

One form of power that humans have always wanted and continue to strive for is power over nature. Humans are constantly trying to mimic and control their environment. For example, humans build massive dams and nuclear power stations, they interfere with weather patterns and alter the DNA structure of our food. This manipulation of the natural world gives us a sense of false freedom; we humans believe we're in charge. We become caught up in the wrong notion that having power also gives us control over our environment. We forget that the technologies and things that make us powerful can change in an instant. Our denial of the true power of the natural world has led mankind to the brink of extinction and will do so again. Massive floods, powerful hurricanes and tornadoes, and destructive wild fires have proven time and again to be more powerful than the arrogance of man.

As ridiculous as it may seem, it is almost as if we humans need to be constantly reminded of the importance of the natural world to our existence. Breathable air, wind, fire and clean water are essential if life on Earth is to be sustained. Despite the fact that we know this we continue to poison the water, fill the air with pollutants and throw the Earth out of balance. Essentially, we have taken what is an unbelievably uniquely crafted system that works from the smallest cell to the grandeur of the universe and systematically taken it apart. We should be ashamed.

Raven's experience with humankind left him wounded and resentful. When he asked for the wind to do his bidding he was acting out of revenge for the loss of a family member. Bear understood that Raven felt powerless and wanted to redress the balance. Raven desired the power of humankind so that they would suffer as well. Bear is wise to see that when the balance between nature and humans is tilted toward one or the other then all are in danger.

Almost all indigenous cultures have stories that contain ancient warnings that humans must show respect and reverence for the Earth. These warnings come in the form of prophecies and teachings that include an inherent understanding of the natural order of all things. We humans forget the gravity of our actions when we do not obey the natural order. The desire for balance should always outweigh the need for power and revenge. When we act from a place of anger, fear and reprisal we are automatically out of balance. We are taking the gift of free will and abusing it, crossing a line that can have implications far beyond our understanding. Raven doesn't comprehend the ramifications of asking the wind to change what was the natural order. Instead, he risked the entire forest and all lives that lived in it. Bear knows this, and he seeks a conversation with the wind to redress the balance while at the same time showing compassion for the pain that Raven is experiencing. Bear learns of Raven's love for him when he is shown the vision of being plucked out of the flames and lifted to safety. At the same time Bear must also come to terms with his own anger towards the loss of his parents in the forest fire. The story shows that Bear's ability to ask forgiveness is a true sign of power; one that is not driven by ego, but an understanding and respect for all elements and life on Earth.

6

Dreaming

The bears fell asleep in the sunlight warming their bodies. They felt safe and protected. The sun looked down on the bears and could hear their hearts beating as one. Sun smiled and thanked the Earth for these healers. The Earth smiled back at the Sun and said that they were now ready for their journey. The bears, fast asleep, started to dream the same dream.

They were running from men with guns who were moving in close behind them. The male bear turned to the female bear and said, "Let's call upon the Goddess to help us."

The Earth heard their call. Her energy came up through the sand stirring the air and filling it with dust and leaves. The men were startled. They had to stop to wipe their eyes and cough. The Earth heard one of them say, "We must get those bears; they are threatening my home and my family."

The Earth, who has endless compassion for all who live upon her surface, asked the bears, "Have you threatened their home and family?"

The bears who were still frantically running said, "No! We were trying to get home! We accidentally crossed their path, we did not realize we were not allowed on that land."

The male bear huffed, and said, "How were we to know that the lands have been divided? Humans falsely make claim to the land as their property."

The Earth smiled and said she understood, and that she recognized how easy it would be to wander onto any land and not realize where you are. The bears were becoming exhausted.

'He wrapped his arms around her
and they warmed themselves in the sun.
The dream they shared was for the Earth.
The Sun could hear their hearts beat.'

They heard a loud bang. They stopped and turned around. Way off in the distance at the bottom of a steep ravine they saw a man lying on the ground. He had come from the woods looking for his dog. The hunters mistook him for a bear.

Now, the bears sat beside a log. Tears ran down their faces causing their fur to turn dark and wet. They asked the Earth, "Why can't humans live in harmony with all that live upon her soil?"

She said, "They are not connected to me in the ways that you are. They do not understand the medicine I hold and give to all who live upon me. They become fixated with power because their fear runs wild."

The bears looked at each other, and said, "But we are wild!"

The Earth said, "Exactly, they fear that you are a threat to their lives. If only they could hear my song at night… I sing to them while they sleep. They would learn that if they chose freedom they would have a choice to live in harmony, or to live in fear. Understanding the true nature of my world means accepting the cycle of life."

The bears smiled and thanked the Earth for helping them escape the hunters. The Earth replied, "My medicine created what both sides needed to better understand fear. I do not want harm to come to any of my children."

The bear said, "What about the man who was shot?"

"There is no greater sorrow than mine when a senseless act of violence happens. This man crossed their path and thinking he was a bear, they shot him. They were determined to get revenge. The energy of their fear of bears connected with the man's fear of losing his dog. In this case fear caused both victim and perpetrator."

The Earth wrapped her warmth around the bears. They crawled inside the log and went to sleep.

When the bears awoke they were wrapped in each other's arms, grateful it was just a dream.

Our dream time is often connected to the past. When we dream those dreams can be of places and people we feel attached to or have unresolved conflict with. Dreams can also come from the future but for the most part our dreams are of the past or present. Dream time offers a deeper look into the psyche and allows us to experience what we have not yet resolved. Conscious dreaming takes people into a precognitive state allowing the future to unfold, but this is rare and truly a gift. In the ancient past, cultures around the world revered members of their societies who had the gift of conscious dreaming and they were called *dreamers.* These people remained in a state of dreaming even while awake. This state of consciousness was always accompanied by a deep spiritual practice and the dreamer also had a spiritual guide. The Australian aborigine believe that during dreamtime, a person's entire ancestry exists to guide them, and that all of the knowledge of the world is held by one's ancestors.

One way to interpret dreams is to see ourselves as all the characters in the dream and try to interpret what the characters are trying to convey. Or we can look at the dream from a symbolic point of view and ask ourselves what for example does the dog, boat or ocean represent? In my experience, to dream of a large body of water can indicate that you are deep in your emotional body trying to work something out. Dreaming of bears might indicate that some form of healing is taking place. The important thing to do is to record your dream once you wake up. Then I suggest sitting with the dream in meditation and even ask the Earth to help you understand what that dream was all about.

Where we go and what we do in our dream time is dependent upon how aware we are of our subconscious. I have learned that we are living in **this** reality and many other realities all at the same time, which can open the dreamtime to the past, present and future. The problems you are wrestling with in your life will often show up in your dreams. However, when we are able to achieve peace deep within ourselves we may experience a different kind of dreaming; one that allows us to travel in the space that exists between this world and the next.

'Now it is time to recognize what is yours
and what belongs to others.'

7

The Burden

Every morning she would rise with the Sun, offer her prayers and ask to be shown the way. The Sun was always happy to hear her voice. Then she would gather herbs and plants by the rocks near the forest and speak to nature. She was a medicine woman, and her medicine was strong. She helped the people of her village with her doctoring. But sometimes she could not save the lives of those she treated and while she understood this was part of the natural cycle of life, she carried the people and their pain with her.

Now, she stopped for a moment, put down her basket of herbs and knelt by the creek. She hoped the gentle melody of the water lapping against the rocks would comfort her as it had so often before. Tears fell from her face, dropped into the creek and were carried away. If only the creek would take the pain she felt too. Her path was not an easy one. Then, in the water she saw the reflection of an old friend – Bear.

"Why are you crying?"

She looked up into his eyes and said, "I am sad, I feel so many people in pain, suffering, and I can only do so much."

Bear smiled, "What if you ask Creator to help you?"

"I always ask for help, but I feel responsible for everyone."

Bear's eyes grew wide and gently he said, "It is not for you to carry this burden. Everyone has their own path, with many things to learn, forgive and understand. You call it karma. I call it life."

"How do I let go?"

"You simply ask Creator to take your burden. Lighten your load. This is far bigger than you or any of us. You are a vessel for the Earth and Creator. Remember your healing gifts were given to you by Creator."

She looked down at her hands, "My grandmother was a medicine woman. She taught me everything I know. I do not want to let her down."

Bear's eyes fixed on her as he said, with a serious tone, "This is a big responsibility. You must learn how to carry these things, so you don't crumble under the weight of your basket." He motioned to the basket that sat next her.

Bear opened his medicine bag and took out his drum. He started to sing a song low and rhythmic. Raven landed near the creek, watching, listening. Bear got louder, and she felt the air change and the temperature drop. She saw Bear and Raven and the creek and then a rush of light filled her vision. She was overcome with a sensation of passing through time and space at a rapid speed. She lost consciousness. When she opened her eyes, she could see family members who had passed. She was overwhelmed with emotion and started to cry. They greeted her and shared hugs.

She looked at Bear, "Where are we?"

"You know where we are."

"But how?"

"It is my medicine that brought you here."

"We have crossed the boundaries of this world and gone into the spirit world."

Embracing her, Grandmother said, "I have watched you work and give of your energy to those you doctor and heal. It is important that you remember that you do not have the right to carry the pain of others. It is not yours, and it jeopardizes your wellbeing. This is the most difficult part of being a medicine woman. Trust me, I learned this the hard way." She looked at Bear.

Bear sighed, "I remember many times you took on illness and energy that didn't belong to you, Grandmother. Raven and I had to bring you back from the place ghosts walk."

The painful memory crossed Grandmother's face. She nodded, "It was nearly my death."

"We nearly lost you, we nearly lost you," Raven chimed.

Grandmother looked deep into her granddaughter's eyes, "Bear has brought you here, so you can see all of us. Family, friends, people from the village, everyone is here. Look at our faces and see we are at peace, happy and content to be home. We no longer carry the pain and illness we once had. We are free."

"But that doesn't help anyone at home," she cried. "I am trying to help them out of their pain and suffering." Hot tears burned her cheeks as she spoke.

Grandmother put her arm around her granddaughter, "Your gifts are a blessing and I am proud of you. Now it is time to recognize what is yours and what belongs to others. You can help people, doctor them and love them, but you cannot take their pain. Your heart is generous, and your love runs deep like the river. Protect yourself, value your medicine and have boundaries with illness and disease that can plague the minds and bodies of humans. Remember I am always there, helping you and guiding you."

Seeing her Grandmother, she remembered the time the elder became ill after caring for a sick child in the village. She was only a young girl and the memory of her own mother staying up night after night praying, smoking and calling on the ancient ones was etched into her mind. After nearly dying her Grandmother was rushed to Bear's cave where Bear and Raven brought her back from the ghost realm. It was after that her mother insisted she begin to learn the medicine way from her Grandmother. Tears spilled from her eyes.

She whispered, "Thank you Grandmother, I am happy."

Raven interrupted, "Time to go!"

Bear grabbed his rattle and started singing his song. Lights passed before her eyes and once again she felt a surge of energy pass through her. As she crossed the border between worlds the images of her family faded. Opening her eyes, she found herself back at the creek as if she had never left. Her body was somehow lighter – she felt relieved.

She lit some cedar and used the smoke on her basket. Bear and Raven sat in silence as she emptied the pain and suffering she had been carrying. She asked Creator to take it all. She said she no longer needed to carry other people's burdens. She looked into the river realizing the pain of others is not what defines her but rather being empty allows her more room to grow.

Bear and Raven went back into the woods, smiling.

This story is about the burdens many of us take on in our lives that don't really belong to us. We all have a tendency to blur the lines and boundaries that are naturally in place for each one of us to deal with our own issues, feelings or karma. Our society is riddled with a myriad of dysfunctional behaviors and addictions, ways in which we attempt to deaden not only our own pain but the pain of others. And for some highly sensitive humans, appropriate boundaries around what belongs to them and what does not will become muddled. In some cases, especially for those who consider themselves empaths, the story reflects the inclination to take on other people's complex feelings and emotions. People with extraordinary sensitivity have struggled throughout time with handling the exchange of energies between them and others. For example, it's often possible to become sad and depressed, or filled with anxiety and fear because we are opening ourselves up to, or picking up on, this energy from another person. The universal law that energy begets energy suggests that we will carry that sadness and depression or anxiety and fear within ourselves. It becomes a vibrational match. This is why empaths have such a difficult time discerning what is theirs and what is another person's because ultimately, they are connecting to their own emotional content at a super-high frequency. This makes it even more important that highly sensitive people learn how to ground their energy and not take on the emotions of others. It also becomes clear that all of us need to take responsibility for our own feelings and learn how to ground them.

For me, an empath is someone who feels everything and has a deep connection to a 'gut feeling'. A healer, on the other hand, has not only empathic abilities but is also gifted with other-worldly connections. In this story, the medicine woman is both an empath and a gifted healer who comes from generations of medicine people. She is crying by the river because her basket is filled with other people's pain and sorrow. The metaphor of a basket simply illustrates what many healers take on inappropriately while caring for others; they often take on their patient's emotional baggage as well as the burden and responsibility of healing. In today's world, doctors, surgeons and medical practitioners carry the burden and expectation of healing their patients from illness, disease and sometimes saving their lives in emergency situations. If they are unable to cure or heal someone then healers also experience loss. The death of someone they are caring for is something healers have to come to terms with and realize that it is Creator's will not theirs. By surrendering to a higher power, healers and empaths are more able to manage their emotions so that they are not carrying more than their own.

In the story, the medicine woman's guidance and counsel come from a character that is found both in Norwegian and Native American lore – Bear. He has the wisdom and experience as a medicine man to help her to see the burden she is carrying and the need for her to release it. Bear has magical powers and abilities that far surpass the human realm. The fact that he took her into the spirit realm is indicative of her innate abilities as a medicine woman, and that she is ready for this journey. The experience that she has meeting her family and loved ones who have crossed over and are now free of pain and emotional burdens teaches her that even though in her world she cannot always alleviate pain and suffering there is a place where we are free from human suffering of any kind. Like the Norwegian mythical characters Huginn and Munnin, Raven not only has the ability to see what is going on, but he is also able to transport through the different realms. He is sensitive to what is happening and often cries the warning that is leading to the truth.

Humans have the responsibility to manage their emotional energy. The powerful palette of feelings we inherit at birth can take us places we never thought possible. When we learn to release the burden of not only our own wounds but others we feel we must carry, we begin the real journey.

8

Death

She lay down on the rocks to sleep and the Ravens came to her with their medicine. The Earth was cradling her like a baby. She remembered what it felt like to be held in her mother's arms. She told the Ravens to keep watch over her and to let her know should anyone approach. She closed her eyes. She saw the rocks swirling around her like clouds in the sky. She sang a song she learned from the Earth and asked Creator to help her. Creator looked down upon her and smiled and said, "I am here watching over you. Let your journey begin."

She felt herself leave her body and go up into the sky. She was inside a tunnel of light that made her laugh and feel weightless. She wondered why she hadn't done this sooner. Her body had been riddled with pain. Now she was swirling in an intensely bright light all the time moving higher and higher through the tunnel. And she could see people around her, people she had known during her lifetime. Her parents held out their hands to her and her Grandmother put her arm around her waist drawing her toward her. "Now you are home," she said.

Below her she could see the Ravens — small black specks sitting on stones where her body lay. She smiled. At last she had come to the end of the tunnel of light and she stepped into an aura shimmering with many shades of gold, silver and white. She saw Creator waiting for her and she ran to him and hugged him. She told him how grateful she was that he helped her in her journey. He smiled. "I am happy you have finally come home. I have watched you in your life loving ALL people.

'He kept watch while she entered a new life.'

I have also watched you honor the Earth while also giving up your pain, sorrow and love to her. I have seen you struggle with your feelings of anger and resentment. I know how you have suffered at the hands of those who do not understand you."

She began to cry. She realized how much she had yearned to hear those words. She looked into his eyes and asked if she would ever go back to Earth. Creator said, "Yes you are not done yet and I will prepare you for your next incarnation. It may seem that you have been here for many years, but once you return to Earth you will forget this place."

Her family surrounded her, smiling and asking her if she was ready. Ready for what she wondered? "I just got here," she told her loved ones.

"No!" said one, "You have actually been here for over fifty earthbound years. Time has been a long nap in the warm sun for you."

Once again, a smile came to her face as she remembered the last place she laid down. Like a bird she felt her soul body lift and descend towards Earth. She settled inside the belly of a woman she would soon call her mother. She could see the Ravens dancing above her squawking and welcoming her back to the Earth.

Earth Medicine teaches us about the cycle of life. We plant seeds in the spring and watch them grow. The plants bear fruit and the harvest follows in the late summer and early fall. Then the plants die and return to the soil. We see this cycle of life in every living thing. The Earth provides a constant recycling of her body to ensure life. We can better embrace death if we stay conscious of the cycle and recognize our bodies are of the Earth.

Elizabeth Kubler-Ross suggests we experience 'little deaths' that prepare us for our ultimate journey. These 'little deaths', or completions, such as the finishing of a project, the end of a school year or ultimately the loss of loved ones, are a part of what she calls being in your Autumn's rhythm. Each time we experience a completion it teaches us about the cycle that has ended. As we go through these Earth cycles or seasons we are training for our own Autumn to return to the Earth.

The Earth is constantly teaching us. Everything has a rhythm and a song. The song is often a vibration but on the Earth plane it sounds like music. When we sit quietly in meditation we can hear all kinds of sounds. Life on Earth is busy and often noisy. Find your song. Listen to Earth and hear her share your song with you. It is usually very simple and a short melody you can hum over and over to yourself. This is not a song that has composed words and a complicated score! This is the song of your soul.

There are tribes in Africa that bring their newborns into the world with everyone singing a song that is special for that baby. Everyone knows this song and when the child grows up and has a difficult time the community will sing their song to them. When they go through rites of passage their song is sung. When they die the village sings their song again. This is a great reminder that we all have a song. Learn your song from the Earth. Put your ear close to the ground and ask that she share this with you. Teach your family your song so they can sing this to you when it is time for you to journey across the Milky Way.

Death is nothing more than a passage into the parallel Universe. Our natural state is in spirit form. The only thing keeping us from embracing this passage is fear. The fear of not knowing, of not believing, of not understanding what is unseen. We are infinite as souls and we are having a human experience. Understand this moment in time is a second to what is an immeasurable life. Our passage into the parallel universe is guided. Our relatives wait for us and help us through the tunnel of light all the way to Creator.

There is too much evidence of reincarnation to think this life is all there is. The life we have is precious and should be treated so. There are hundreds and hundreds of lifetimes here on Earth for many souls. Some are new souls coming through to Earth for the first time. Those new souls have had hundreds of lifetimes in other parts of the galaxy and beyond. When we can find peace within ourselves and trust our soul is infinite, we can better embrace this passage called Death.

'He came for her disguised as a bear,
hoping no one would notice.'

9

The Illusion

She was hiding in the mountains making her home in the rocks and trees. She wanted a new life, a new beginning. She was strong and independent. Although she was alone, she had many friends in the stones that circled her camp as well as the deer, squirrels and rabbits that visited on a regular basis. Even the moon kept an eye on her.

She had a hurt that ran so deep it felt as if the ocean was inside of her. Her tears would run down her cheeks for days on end. When she was young she had been betrayed and abandoned by her father. He told her he would never leave her, but then one day he left and never came back. Though her memories were fading, the hurt stayed fresh.

She experienced it all over again with a man she swore she would love until the end of time. Her hurt festered and she wore it like a badge on her chest. She would talk about the injustice and betrayal she felt to her friends in the forest. One day, after the birds sang their morning song, a bear came to visit. She was delighted to see this new friend. He asked her how she was feeling, and he confessed that he had heard her crying. Lowering her eyes, she told him she felt depressed and lonely because she had just lost the love of her life. The bear wrapped his arms around her and comforted her. They grew close spending everyday together talking and laughing and walking through the forest.

One day the bear whispered in her ear, "I want you to see something." She followed him into the woods where a family of bears played and basked in the sun. They smiled and said, "Please join us." The bear was happy his family accepted her. They spent time eating and talking with them. She spent time with the bear and his family each day and grew closer and closer to her new friend.

Raven came and sat on her head. He told her that the bear was not who she thought he was. "What do you mean?" she cried. The bear turned and looked at her. She could see the edges of his fur glimmering as if she was looking at him through the bright sunlight. She gasped and watched the bear turn into a man.

"Who are you?" she asked. The bear told her he was sent to her by the mountain she lived under. The mountain heard her crying and knew her heart had been broken. The mountain wanted to ease her pain and help her to heal her heart. The bear, who had now fully transformed into a man, stood before her and said, "The illusion of my true form is not meant to deceive you but rather allow you to love again and not be afraid."

She stood and looked him deep in the eyes. She recognized the same feeling she had had when she looked into the bear's eyes. She took his hand. They walked to the clearing and sat down together. Still holding his hand, she thanked him for helping her to heal her heart and believe she could love again. The man embraced her.

As they held one another she felt a stirring inside. She whispered, "What is happening?" The Raven on her head cackled and said, "You are changing." She felt her arms get thicker, her legs stronger and her sense of smell became amplified. She looked down and saw that her arms were covered with fur as were his. She jumped back and yelped. She was a bear.

They stood there in the meadow looking at each other. She said, "How can this be?"

"You were ready to heal and transform your life into what you truly wanted," he answered. She felt her mouth pull back into a smile and they walked happily together into the woods.

What is the illusion? It is everything that we create here on Earth. We live in a constant state of emotional creation or illusion. It is my belief that our emotional body exudes vibrations, which travel through time and space and meet up with like-minded energies. Sometimes we recreate karma or emotional wounds from our past lives producing the illusion that we are back in the same *feeling* again. Our belief systems contribute to how we create the illusions. We continually manifest templates of what we want to believe, and we stick to them. This creates an energy cycle that goes out into the universe and comes back to us as matched energy.

The illusion only exists if we allow it. In the story the girl is alone and, in her sorrow, has made friends with the bear. She allowed herself to open up emotionally and love again and from that experience discovered *she* was the illusion. By letting go of our belief systems we become present and available to see beyond the illusion.

Earth energy delivers a like vibration to humans based on their intentions. Good intentions and sincerity aligns with the Earth and Creator allowing for a real experience not an illusion. It takes practice and dedication to live outside of the ego.

For example, a person seeking wealth and riches might work hard and save to buy cars, jewelry and clothes, but while doing so they buy into the illusion created by society of how they should look, what they should wear and what car to drive. This template is the doctrine people follow because it is the popular choice.

In all the stories in Norse mythology, the character of Loki has the hardest time facing his own ego. His intentions can be good and aligned with the demi gods and at other times he is deceitful and menacing. He creates illusions to play tricks on others and accomplish his own agenda. He is driven by his ego and unhealthy behavior like the trickster coyote, but his meddling always gets him into trouble. His character teaches us that the illusion does not last because no matter what he has done the truth is always revealed and therein lies the teaching.

The ego is a magical firewall that exists to protect us. When we are healthy and living close to the Earth, uninhibited by the illusion, the ego will function in an appropriate manner. But when we are living in a state of addiction and unhealthy behavior we create the false ego. This can take us into the illusion even further by building invisible barriers that keep us from facing the truth. The false ego must go through a death for us to return to a natural state of being. This can be painful because most people do not want to feel their belief systems have failed them.

A daily practice of grounding our energy into the Earth, sharing our stories with her and being grateful for what we have while asking for little, helps us to learn to see through the veil. We are living in the fifth dimension which makes it critical that we choose to live closer to the Earth. This higher frequency has brought about a shift in humanity that is pushing mankind toward an awakened state. But we will still wrestle with the illusion which is why healing our karma has never been so important. Sometimes the search for higher consciousness leads people off track which can result in addictions such as shopping, gaming, sex, alcohol, drugs and more. The human experience can often be so overwhelming that instead of obtaining the true nature of these higher energies through practices like meditation we reach for instant gratification. To return to a natural state of being we must confront our addictions, belief systems and the ego.

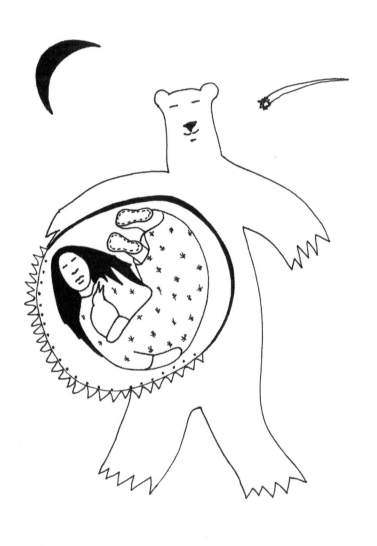

'Bear kept her in his drum.'

10

A Safe Place

Bear could feel the Earth's heartbeat as he sang songs about the land, the four-legged, winged ones and the stars in the sky. Each song was blessed with his love and dedication for the Earth.

One day, Bear saw a shooting star cross the sky and fall down to Earth. He wondered if his song called the star from the sky. He thought he better go check it out and see what had fallen to the planet. Bear traveled far and wide singing and drumming the whole way. Finally, he reached the place where the star touched the Earth.

The moon shone bright and encouraged him to look closer. There in the middle of a crater sat a girl. She was singing a song that Bear knew! He said, "Excuse me, how do you know that song?"

She looked up at Bear and smiled. She said, "I have known this song since before the beginning of time. This song came from the Earth. I have visited this planet many times since you were born and have heard you singing her songs and drumming them into the Universe. I was happy you came to find me."

Bear was delighted and walked into the crater helping her to her feet. He carried her up the steep slope and into the cool grassy field. When he looked into her eyes he could see the Universe sparkling back. He blinked and looked again; there it was, all of the constellations in her eyes. He gasped, "Who are you?"

She said, "I am like the Earth. I have traveled around the galaxy listening to all the different songs of the planets and the sun. Your songs were the loudest and carried a vibration of love so immense I had to meet you."

Bear blushed and told her he loved the Earth more than life itself. He had dedicated his life to her songs and drumming her heartbeat into the sky. The girl said that she wanted to meet the voice they had all come to know in the galaxy and beyond. He looked at her and asked, "How would my voice be different from the other voices who carry her songs and drum her heartbeat?"

She said, "You have dedicated your life to her, that is the difference. You understand that the Earth has a soul and a purpose. You also understand that you are a caretaker of this beautiful planet and your life is dependent upon hers."

Bear teared-up and said, "Yes I feel all of those things. I want to help her and sing to her the songs she has taught me."

The girl smiled and told Bear she wanted to sing with him. Bear starting drumming and singing the song he had heard at the crater. Their voices blended together, and Bear could feel Earth energy swirling up all around them like the woven blankets his mother used to keep him warm. He closed his eyes singing at the top of his lungs, happier than he had ever felt. When the song ended he opened his eyes and the girl was gone.

He cried out for her as he ran around the field looking into the crater where he had found her. He sat down and cried. His tears pooled on the soft soil. All of sudden he heard her voice, "I am here Bear. I am inside your drum. I will be with you until the end of time."

Bear held up his drum to the moonlight and could see her image through the skin of the drum! She had Raven with her. Bear quickly asked Raven, how did YOU get in there?"

Raven cackled, "I have always been here. I am your drum."

Bear saw the Raven's black feathers glimmering in the moonlight on the rim of the instrument. He cried out, "Please don't take my drum, Raven!"

Raven replied, "How could I take myself away from the truth that you sing about the Earth?"

Bear held the drum tight and the girl's voice rose out of the drum with a new song. Bear stood up to learn this song and soon he was singing along with her. He made his way home singing and drumming with a new sense of purpose. Bear felt the Universe was much closer to him than the distant stars he once sang about.

It is important to have a safe place to go. For some it is home or a special place in the garden. For other's it is a visit to Grandma's house where the smell of fresh baked bread and pies creates a sense of safety and love. It's different for everyone but there is one safe place we can all access with ease through meditation and that is the special place within ourselves.

When I meditate I like to think of myself as a tree connecting with the energy of the Earth at my feet and the flow of the Creator coming into the top of my head. My etheric arms are the branches reaching up to the sky and my legs and feet the roots traveling deep into the ground. The energy of the Earth and Creator fill up my body and all of its energy centers giving me a sense of safety. It is the antidote to our modern life spent in cars and planes moving about at high speeds. This kind of practice helps to lower the blood pressure, improve health and free us from anxiety. Once you have practiced the grounding meditation you can go within and create a place of safety for a lifetime.

Ideally our families provide children with a sense of safety and reassurance but it's not always the case. Emotional wounds and karmic threads from past lives can instead create a variety of negative experiences leaving a child feeling consistently unsafe. That feeling can continue into adulthood and we experience it first hand with the inner child. We look for safety outside of ourselves creating a multitude of situations that can lead to disappointment and fear. We forget that our sense of safety actually comes from within us but often we choose to anchor into the illusion.

Exercise: Find a place to sit down - inside or outside - and close your eyes. Become the tree. Grow your roots deep into the Earth and let your branches reach high into the sky. Find the center of your body right around the heart. Let your consciousness settle there. This is called the soul body. Feel your breath expand your belly and rib cage and let the exhale be slower than the inhale. Feel the space deep inside the soul body. This is home. This is where we came from and where we are returning to. It is the part of us that is always connected to Creator. Take time to sit in this space and fill your heart and mind with the peace you feel inside of you.

11

The Medicine Path

The young girl was always destined to walk a medicine path. She was a sixth-generation healer on her father's side of the family. Her Grandmother taught her father and now he was to teach her. But she was only concerned with chasing Raven as he swooped and squawked through the forest and into the village. She would follow Raven wherever he went. The girl was extremely gifted – she could settle a storm and bring rain to the land. Her parents worried for her safety because she was extremely vulnerable.

"She is just a girl," her mother would say, and her father would reply, "Yes and she is very gifted, we must keep her safe."

Raven called to the girl. She ran off into the woods following her friend. Bear met them at the meadow. He stopped the pair as they played without a care. Bear told the girl it was time.

"Time for what?" she asked seating herself on a mossy rock.

She looked up at Bear who met her gaze. Then she stammered and blurted out, "I don't know what to do with all the information that comes into my head." She told Bear that she could hear the wind, talk to the clouds and feel the pain of her people. Sometimes, she told him, she even felt and saw strange things, but she didn't know what they were.

Bear told the girl that he understood and then he motioned for her to climb on board his back. She giggled with excitement and squiggled onto the Bear's back. She smiled and thought, what would my father think if he could see me now?

Bear started moving across the meadow and into the woods

'If you understand this, you will accept that
all things change and are never stagnant.'

carrying the girl on his back. He walked into a canyon toward an outcropping of rocks. All the stones bore a circular design and were smooth and worn and standing in a perfect circle.

"What is this place?"

"I have brought you to a gathering of healers."

"But I don't know anything, I'm just a child." The girl was afraid and held on tight to Bear's fur.

"Don't worry, I am at your side," Bear reassured her with a smile. He moved towards the center of the circle and the girl could feel energy bubbling up from the ground and surrounding them. Suddenly there were more bears all seated in the circle and the stones appeared to be bigger and tower over them.

"What is happening?" asked the girl.

"The stone circle is a portal from our world to another," Bear said in a hushed voice. The girl scanned the circle and could see bears of all colors and sizes. The circle was made up of 12 large stones with an opening between each megalith. The bears were staring at the girl.

The caramel colored bear spoke first, "Why have you brought her here?"

Bear said, "She is ready to learn."

Bear nudged the girl off his back and told her to stand next to him. Her knees wobbled as she stood to the left of Bear.

The dark brown bear spoke next, "What is your name child?"

She whispered, "Freya."

"Good, now that we know your name, are you ready?"

She looked over at Bear and shrugged, "Yes."

Drums began beating and echoing throughout the circle. The bears started singing. Freya felt warm and flushed. Raven appeared suddenly handing her a sprig of sage, "Follow me!" he exclaimed. She ran towards Raven, but her legs felt heavier than usual and it was difficult to catch up with the bird. Her legs scrambled under her and she thought she would fall. When she looked down she saw that her legs were covered in fur. She was a bear!

"Wait, Raven!"

Raven stopped and landed by her side. "What is wrong Freya?"

"I am a bear! How did this happen? Where is Bear and the others?"

"Ooh so many questions. Follow me!"

Freya lumbered along on four legs followed by Raven. Eventually, they came to her home. But something was wrong – her father was not home, and her mother was very old.

"What happened here?"

"This is the future. You are seeing what is to come."

"But why?" she cried. "I don't want to see this." Freya looked away.

Raven looked deep into her eyes and said, "Freya, you have a special gift. If you understand this, you will accept that all things change and are never stagnant. You will understand that your ability to transform into a bear is how you will learn from Bear and the council. I am showing you what the future holds for you. Come with me."

Raven led the girl into the house. Then Freya saw a grown woman walk into the living room and realized she was looking at her future self. She was long, lean and strong. Freya watched as she took herbs from a basket and doctored her mother. One by one people she did not know came to the house and she attended to them with healing and herbs. Freya looked at Raven, "I am busy as an adult."

"Yes, you are little one, you are sought after from far and wide."

Raven motioned for her to follow him from the house back to the woods. They arrived at the stone circle and she could see a

*big brown bear waiting for them. "Who is that?" she whispered
to Raven.*

"You'll see!" he squawked.

*Moments later she began to transform from her bear body
back to her human form. She entered the circle and the singing and drumming stopped. The Bear at the edge of the woods
returned to his place in the circle.*

*Raven spoke, "In order for you to do the work you have ahead
of you it was important that we show your future. Take your
training seriously and respect your elders."*

*Bear added, "You need first to be a child Freya. We want you
to understand that we are here to help. Right now, you're too
young to accept the burdens you will carry as an adult. Those
burdens are not meant for you now."*

*She looked at each one of the bears and Raven and asked,
"When will I begin my training?"*

Raven cackled, "You already have."

*Bear had her climb up onto his back once again and they took
their leave of the council and the circle of stones.*

*"You can always return to the stone circle and find the coun-
cil whenever you need them."*

*She hugged Bear tight as they made their way home. Her
father was waiting for her at the edge of the woods. She looked at
him with surprise. "Were you at the council in the stone circle?"*

*Her father replied, "Yes dear. I was there. I waited for you at
the edge of the woods when Raven showed you the future." He
thanked Bear and Raven for her safe return.*

"Why didn't you tell me?"

*Her father replied, "I wanted you to see for yourself. It is
much more powerful if you see these things with your own eyes."*

*She took her father's hand as they walked back to her family
home – she felt loved and secure and she hoped this moment
would never end.*

The Norwegians call their gifted medicine people healers or shamans or Noaidi. Native Americans refer to them as a medicine man or woman. The medicine path is a difficult one. There is nothing glamorous about being a healer, these people give only of themselves and never ask for anything in return. They are rare men and women who often undergo spiritual tests that shape the nature of their work. One of the biggest tests of all is the death of the ego and the transformation from self-realization to becoming god-realized. Many healers do not make it past the earthbound tests remaining engaged in glamor and self-importance and only a few become self-realized. If they remain true to their calling and surrender to Creator, they experience several deaths of the ego. As this process happens it is common for them to be tested again and again. These painful passages in their lives are what help to make them understand the human condition. Many people would like the gifts of those that walk the medicine path, but they do not realize what it takes for these people to maintain and care for their abilities.

The modern Western world of medicine is fraught with extraordinary expectations of those who work as doctors especially because they are often portrayed in television and movies as super heroes who are able to deliver what in reality are unrealistic outcomes. Those who work in Western medicine go through intense training and study that comes with a price in the same way that shamans, healers and those following the medicine path do. Doctors are known for the savior syndrome. They save lives through medicine, surgery and techniques that have proven their worth in a Western medicine setting. This kind of experience can alter the psyche of the practitioner, often giving a false sense of power. The ego plays a big part in Western medicine, and equally has its grips on healers, shamans and medicine men.

The path of the medicine man or woman requires being in service and putting others' well-being before their own. It also demands they have clear boundaries and practice self-care. We see this with Bear who is constantly helping others with doctoring and healing. Naturopaths, acupuncturists and herbalists share a connection to Earth Medicine, and like shamans, healers and medicine people their path is directly related to the Earth; they are dedicated to the true nature of doctoring. To be a medicine man or woman requires a combination of gifts and skills that is often derived from teachings passed down through a family member or a mentor. For most, the teachings are based on ones passed down through the clan, family lineage or the particular tribe the healer was born into. The medicine path requires understanding of the physical, mental, emotional and spiritual bodies. The most gifted healers have innate qualities that cannot be mimicked or made up.

Freya's father and mother are determined that she have a childhood and that they do not place adult responsibilities on her. Children not only want to be loved, cherished, valued and respected, but it is up to the parents to gauge what age is appropriate for the child. Clearly Freya has immense ability and is fortunate to have parents that recognize that and do not want to abuse it. Through their own experience, Freya's parents are acutely aware of the path of the healer and how important it is that one is not emotionally wounded when

tending to others. As Freya faces the future, and a life of healing, she is surrounded by the support of her parents and the
council of bears. Not many people have such support. Those
who walk the medicine path are chosen for their karmic abilities with lifetimes of experience built into their DNA. While
some claim to possess intuitive insight and healing gifts, in
reality, true healers are few and far between.

12

What Deer Had to Say...

Raven flew over the forest, looking for Bear. "Deer needs your help!" he squawked.

Bear heard Raven, grabbed his medicine bag and ran off to look for Deer. When he found her, Deer was laying on her side. Her breathing was labored, and she was shaking. Bear took out his rattle and began to sing a healing song.

As he sang a beautiful woman appeared. She stood over Deer, "I am the Keeper of Deer Medicine and I have come to help you," she said.

"Thank you," nodded Bear reverently, "I was hoping you would come."

The Keeper of Deer Medicine knelt over Deer's quivering body and rubbed her limbs with a gold powder. Then she blew the powder in the four directions – above and below. Her magic was strong. Bear kept singing and watching. Raven was in the tree making loud noises in his throat and clicking and clacking to the rhythm of the song.

The Keeper of Deer Medicine told Bear, "Deer can see the future and it has brought illness to her physical body."

She pulled stringy webs out of Deer's legs and back. "She has seen something that was difficult for her to understand."

Bear looked at the beautiful woman, "What can I do to help her?"

"Stay with her. Keep her warm. She will come back to you and when she does, listen to her story. Then go to the edge of the forest and await my instructions."

*'I had a vision about the future
and when I fell I saw the Keeper of
Deer Medicine standing over me.'*

Bear nodded in agreement. Then he asked Raven to fetch a blanket while he built a fire. Raven flew off into the forest and returned with the warmest blanket he could find in Bear's cave. They followed the Keeper of Deer Medicine's instructions and wrapped Deer in the woolen blanket.

Night fell and slowly Deer's family began to appear around the camp. Bear continued his vigil singing his song over her. Eventually, Deer stirred groggily. She sat up. "Where am I?"

"You are in my camp," said Bear. "Raven told me you needed help."

"Thank you Bear. I always knew you would come. I had a vision about the future and when I fell I saw the Keeper of Deer Medicine standing over me." Bear lowered his voice, "She was here," he said. "Please, tell me of your vision."

Deer began, "We were running through the woods; a great fire burned at the south end. The sky was filled with ash and smoke. The forest creatures ran together, deer, bear, hawk, raven, squirrel, rabbit. We ran for our lives. The humans were at war with one another. They were destroying the Earth. I became paralyzed by what I was witnessing. I feared we would lose everything. When the vision ended I became ill. That is when Raven saw me fall." Bear could see from the look on Deer's face that she knew she had had a vision of the future and what would come to pass.

Bear said, "We must go to the edge of the forest." Bear packed up his medicine bag and together he and Raven helped Deer to her feet and they began their journey to the edge of the woods. Raven flew overhead calling out for them to hurry.

In a meadow near a large outcrop of trees they saw The Keeper of Deer Medicine waiting for them. Upon their arrival she ushered them quickly to the center of the grassy area where a great grey stone stood. The Keeper of the Deer Medicine looked at Bear and said gravely, "We must all travel back to change this if we are to prevent what Deer saw in her vision."

Deer's family retreated to wait in the trees and watch as Bear, Raven, Deer and the Keeper all disappeared. It was as if they walked right through the stone. It was a portal that carried them back in time. Bear knew of this kind of travel and he held on to Deer as they swooshed through a long tunnel. When they emerged the Earth was quiet, there were no noises from the modern world. The Keeper said, "Follow me."

They began to walk. Bear saw a giant tree ahead of them. "I know this place," he said, "I have visited this tree before."

Bear began to speak to the tree in his ancient language. A massive doorway opened up in the tree's trunk. They entered and followed the winding stairs that led down to the center of the Earth. They came upon a dimly lit cavern with lanterns around the outer edge. A fire burned in the center of the space. They gathered around it.

Bear spoke his ancient language to the flame, "We have come from the future and need your help. Deer had a terrifying vision of our future. Our forest is in grave danger."

The fire flickered and became brighter. A powerful voice rose out of the flame, "Mankind will try to destroy this planet. The Earth and all the elements have known this since the beginning of time."

The Keeper of Deer Medicine spoke, "We are asking for your help."

Suddenly, the fire grew enormous. They jumped back. In a loud voice the fire said, "You presume this course of action is not correct?"

The Keeper, Bear, Raven and Deer all whispered. "Yes!"

"Then you have presumed something that you do not understand correctly."

They looked at each other puzzled by the fire's statement.

"We cannot change what must come to pass. The destruction of the forest is part of the learning humans must go through. You, the

animals are from another spirit. You do not possess the destructive nature of humans. You were put on Earth to help and teach them."

Raven blurted out, "But we do not want to die and lose our home because of their stupidity."

The fire became soft and playful, "You are not going to die Raven, you and the animals will survive."

The Keeper suddenly looked as if she understood. "The portals," she said quietly.

"Yes," the fire hissed, licking the edge of the logs.

Bear looked at The Keeper and said, "In Deer's dream we were all running for the portal!"

"Yes!" The Keeper said, dropping an offering onto the fire. Flames shot into the air for an instant and then settled back into the body of the fire. Once again, the fire spoke. "Understand the lessons of mankind are not the lessons of the animal kingdom. Deer's vision is important, so you remain alert and ready. There is life everywhere in the Universe. This is not the only sanctuary for the animals." The fire grew. The cavern lit up, "Now you must go back. Understand that when the time comes, you will return home. It is there that you will understand the lessons that you helped Creator provide for mankind."

Bear had tears in his eyes, "There are some humans we are attached to and feel loss and pain over this lesson they must learn."

"You will meet them again. There is no end to this Universe and the life that exists everywhere."

Raven let out a series of clicks and clacks saying, "We must trust Creator."

The flames died down and the fire appeared to go out for a split second, like a pause in the middle of a breath. Then it came roaring back, "You are right Raven. Trust and believe in the reality that spans far beyond Earth that is always part of Creator's plan."

Then the fire addressed the Keeper of Deer Medicine. "You who are the Keeper must carry the message to all of the animal kingdom."

She nodded and motioned to the doorway. They thanked the fire with their sacred offerings of cedar and tobacco and returned to the portal. They arrived once again in the meadow and stood in the shadow of the great stone. They were tired and needed to rest. The Keeper of Deer Medicine said, "Thank you for going with me. I am happy to learn what must be done regarding Deer's vision. Now we must trust that Creator has a plan for all of us and that the humans are learning their lessons. We shall continue to provide healing for them." She looked at Bear, Raven and Deer and said, "I must go." And with a blink of the eye she turned back into a deer and ran off into the woods.

Deer saw her family waiting on the edge of the forest. She thanked Bear for his medicine and gracefully trotted off after the Keeper. Bear and Raven sang a healing song for the humans as they headed home.

Precognition is a rare gift. When we have visions of the future it can be frightening and quite unsettling much like Deer's dream in the story. Scientists and researchers deny the existence of precognition and yet it is everywhere in every culture. In Native American tradition someone with this kind of gift would be advising at a high level and in fact, the tribe would often be led by the person having these visions. The Norse took dreams and precognition very seriously. They believed that dreams could foretell the future. One of the most famous examples of this is the dream of the 9th Century Queen Ragnhild of Southern Norway who dreamt of her family's rise to power in the country. In the dream she is said to have removed her broach and held it out in front of herself, so she could get a closer look at it. As she was holding the broach, roots and branches shot out of it reaching the ground and becoming so tall that she could not see beyond it. The branches spread far and wide covering the whole of Norway. This dream became the realization that her son and his heirs would become future rulers of Norway. The dream also depicts Yggdrasill, or the tree of life, and is said to connect to the nine realms.

Hopis also believe there are nine realms. The giant tree in the story of *What Deer Had to Say* is symbolic of the tree of life. As with many sources of knowledge in mythology only a few creatures have access to it and in this case, it is Bear who regularly visits the tree knowing the ancient language to enter. Yggdrasill is at the center of Norse mythology. Its power is well understood by the Norse gods, as is what will befall anyone who misuses the tremendous power held within it.

The tree of life is also symbolic of the elaborate cosmic web or grid that all the planets, stars and life in the universe exist within. Just as sap flows through the branches of a tree feeding each and every limb and leaf, human thoughts and feelings travel as vibrations throughout the grid. These vibrations are connecting with like energies; building blocks for our future. Humans have a responsibility to understand that their love, their fear, their hate, their joy all impact the grid. By remaining unconscious to the power of our emotions we run the risk of creating a dark future. In the story, the animals learn that Deer's vision of a catastrophic event cannot be changed. There are certain events that are formed as a result of the mix of energies on the grid that humans must ultimately take responsibility for and learn from.

Faced with this kind of terrifying vision of the future people of all faiths turn to Creator. In the Hopi way we ask for help from the Gods. We understand through prophesies that this fourth world will come to an end and that the fifth world will follow. In my own teachings, I explain what happened when the Mayan Calendar ended, and we shifted from the fourth dimension into the fifth and the impact on the entire cosmos. We have survived this transition from the fourth dimension into the fifth. It is rare to find a group of people like the Hopi who have full acceptance of these shifts. They trust that traveling from one world to the next is all part of the Creator's plan – they understand there are powers much greater than ourselves at work.

In the story, Bear communicates with the fire which is in fact the voice of Creator. The ancient people respected fire and understood it was very powerful. Mankind has tried to harness and obtain this energy but has learned over centuries that it is impossible. No matter what form we envision Creator as, the fact remains the elements that exist here on Earth are powerful and governed not only by the planet but by a much greater force.

In essence Creator has the big picture and what we might think the solution or what should be done is not necessarily what is best for everyone. What this story tells us is that we have to be responsible for our own energy and its impact on the grid. It is vital that we feel our feelings, process, and release them while grounding our energy into the Earth. Our experience of the future depends on us.

13

Love

Bear was roaming the woods searching for his mate. He had picked up her scent and caught a glimpse of her golden-brown fur through the trees. She was beautiful. He hid among the trunks of the trees, so she wouldn't see him. Raven flew overhead crying out as they drew closer to one another. The wind shifted, and she caught a whiff of his scent. She cooed, "Come out Bear, I know you are near."

Stepping forward bear puffed up his fur, so he looked bigger. "How have you been Mama Bear?" That was his pet name for her, especially when he wanted to be in her good favor.

"You seem to be gone all the time... I am just fine," she replied.

Bear realized he had been on the road for months. His duty as a medicine man meant that he traveled day and night to help those in need. He hung his head, looked at his feet and began to burble an explanation.

She held up her paw, "No need to tell me of your travels. I know you are helping others."

Raven had landed on the tree next to them. "I have something for you," he squawked.

He looked at Mama Bear, "These are from a place down south – a gift for you."

Bear whispered, "Where did you get those?" Raven winked and flew off.

Together they examined two beautiful blankets woven from the finest threads. When they reached their home, it was nearly

'Our love is based on the truth of who we are.'

nightfall. They laid down to rest and covered themselves with the blankets. Mama Bear spoke, "I know you are needed and do fine work, but I am lonely and spend my days missing you."

"I am sorry to be gone so long. I hope I can make it up to you."

They snuggled closer and Bear wrapped his arms around her and they drifted off to sleep. When they woke up the next morning they were both cold, so they grabbed the blankets for warmth. In that moment, they caught sight of one another and screamed!

"Ahhh, you are a human!" Panicked they looked at their bodies. Sure enough, they were no longer bears.

Mama Bear said, "Is this one of Raven's tricks? Where is he? When I get my hands around that scrawny neck..."

Bear stood up and admired his human form. "I am not bad looking as a man," he snorted.

Mama Bear jumped to her feet. She wobbled, "Oops. I am not used to standing on two feet."

They ran around their cave giggling and laughing.

"What will we do as humans?" cried Mama Bear.

"First things first!" Bear took her in his arms and smelled her skin. "Mmm, you smell good!"

And then with a quizzical look on his face he said, "What medicine are these blankets to turn us into humans?"

Raven made a gurgling sound outside the cave to let them know he was there.

Mama Bear went tearing after Raven grabbing at his feathers and yelling, "What have you done? You mangy old bird."

"I have done nothing but provide you with beautiful blankets. What happened to you?"

"That is what I want to know," said Bear.

They gathered moss and asked the resident squirrel to weave them clothes.

"It will cost you, nuts and acorns," she told them. Nervously and with haste the squirrel spun the moss and made coverings for

the transformed bears. Now as humans they were adorned with pants and shirts. They packed the blankets into a bag and headed off south towards the place Raven had acquired the gifts.

The trio stopped along the way, ate food, rested and frolicked in the river nearby. Bear and Mama Bear laughed and chased each other enjoying the use of two legs. Raven chuckled watching them enjoy their human forms.

They arrived in the evening of the following day.

An old woman met them at the base of a tree, where an outcrop of rocks jutted over a cliff. She smiled as they approached.

"Ah humans," she cooed. Her voice was rich. Her hair spun like silver. She wore a long coat and boots that appeared as worn as the rocks.

"Come. Come. It's nice to see you Raven," she said. They followed her path between two rocks and over a crevice through which they could see the forest hundreds of feet below. Her cave was filled with many herbs and strange objects hanging from the ceiling.

"Who have you brought to me?"

Raven sputtered and croaked, "My friends, Bear and Mama Bear. What have you done to them?"

Raven revealed the blankets, pulling them out of the bag.

"Oh, those blankets are for shape-shifters. Do they not want to be shape-shifters?"

Bear replied, "We are happy to be Bears. We have enjoyed our time as humans, but we would rather be in our own bodies."

She chuckled and said, "You're a medicine man, why wouldn't you want to take the disguise of another?"

Bear looked at his arms and legs and said, "Because this body can't do what I am able to do, nor does it have the sustainability of my Bear nature."

Mama Bear chimed in, "If we had wanted to change forms we would have done so with our inner magic."

The old woman paused, "Inner magic… what is that?"

Bear looked at her and demanded they be changed back.

Raven squawked and said, "Change them, change them."
He always repeated himself when he felt nervous.

The old woman took a jar of powder from a shelf behind her and threw a handful of the contents towards Bear and Mama Bear. But in that moment a gust of wind blew through the opening of the cave, picking up the powder with it and depositing it across the face of the old woman. She turned into a badger.

"Oh dear!" She cried out. The two bears stood in their rightful bodies and gasped. "You aren't human at all!"

"No," she admitted. "I am not. I am a Badger." She muttered under her breath and grabbed the blankets. Quickly she wrapped up in them and returned to her human form.

Bear asked, "Why do you choose the human form?"

"I want to walk among the people and feel respected. My kind have been killed off and mistreated. It is my way of preserving our medicine and maintaining my culture."

Bear knew the badgers were healers. He had respect for those he had met in his travels. "I am happy we were able to return the blankets to you," he said.

The old woman replied, "I gave them to Raven, he told me he wanted to be human."

The bears looked at Raven. Together they asked, "What?"

"I didn't mean anything by it", stammered Raven. "I only wanted to try and see what it was like." He turned away, so no one would see his embarrassment.

Bear told the old woman that he and his wife appreciated the opportunity to be humans for a couple days, but they felt more comfortable in their own skin. "Our love is based on the truth of who we are, not disguising ourselves to be something else," he told her.

She nodded. She went back to her jars, this time producing a bundle of herbs. "I want you to have these for all your troubles with my medicine."

Bear asked, "What are you giving us, old woman?"

She smiled. "Love," she said.

Raven made funny noises in his throat. "Love? They have love, why would they need more? I am the one who needs love!"

The old woman smiled and winked at Raven.

Bear put the herbs in his bag. The trio bid the old woman farewell.

On their way home, they stopped once more by the river to rest. Bear pulled the bundle of herbs from his bag and smelled it. His heart swelled with the most incredible sensation of love. He waved the bundle in front of Mama Bear who took a whiff and giggled. He placed it in front of Raven. The bird nibbled at the herbs and fell over with a caw slipping from his beak.

Bear and Mama Bear felt their hearts weave together, stronger than ever with a love they knew could only come from Creator. Bear told Mama Bear that he would never leave her side and she told him that she would always be there for him. Raven was still flat on his back, his wings spread wide. "I love you," he told the bears. They smiled knowing this magic was real.

The search for love is one all humans, throughout lifetimes, have experienced. I believe, that we have not only lived multiple lives experiencing love as both genders, but we search for those connections in each lifetime. It is our reason for being. We look for love believing we have to alter ourselves in some way in order to attract it, when in fact we need to be loved for who we are.

Love can never be disguised as anything else because we are love at the core of our being. This is the lesson of Badger and Bear. Bear is more comfortable being himself. Badger needs to be validated and acknowledged. She thinks taking human form will give her that. Often, the need to be valued and acknowledged is an emotional wound many of us carry. We can try on other looks, hair color, eye color, make up, clothing, muscles and more, but the inner self remains the same. That is the authentic part of you. Being comfortable in your own skin is how we open to divine love. If you are not comfortable with who you are then a series of disguises cannot cover up the pain. When I talk to people on the other side who have passed away, they often tell me their conversation with Creator is not about what they accomplished in life, but rather how much they loved and were loved. This is profound for the millions of people who want to identify with what they have become rather than their true nature.

We share love through our energy. Love is the most powerful vibration uniquely traveling across time and space. When we feel like we cannot find love we must examine our emotional wounds at their deeper roots. Our parents who loved us and gave us a home, may not have had a full understanding of love themselves. This can leave us looking to fill a void created at a young age. Raven felt that he would have a better chance of attracting love by taking human form. When he nibbles at the herbs the old woman gave to Bear he experiences being overwhelmed with the feeling of love. This reminds us that we must love ourselves first before we alter or change anything in search of love outside of ourselves. Sometimes it is difficult to love ourselves. Between our karma, emotional wounds and our soul journey we can spend much of our time like a squirrel chasing our tails. Our soul journey is about raising our consciousness while inhabiting the human form. The mission is to love at the deepest level of your being. This means the most important task you have as a human is to love. It means that through love you will raise your consciousness and evolve this human species.

Love is best understood through experience. We love one another as family, friends, partners and neighbors. Hopefully, we receive love from our parents and learn to love from their example. When we feel lonely or believe that there is no love for us in this world we would be wise to remember that the greatest love comes from Creator. The most important thing any of us can do is love. We should love everyone around the world as much as we love our own family. It is through love we will be liberated as a species.

14

The River's Edge

The girl with many ravens was invited to travel with Bear. He was a medicine man and she had always wanted to go on the road with him. She asked if she could bring her ravens.

"I wouldn't have it any other way," he exclaimed.

The young girl packed her bags quickly and told her ravens to get ready too. They squawked and clicked as they gathered around her.

"It's time to go!" Bear said appearing out of nowhere. The girl with many ravens took his paw in one hand and held on tightly to her bags with the other. She winked at her ravens and off they went.

Together they traveled through the woods to the river's edge. She was tired, and she told Bear she needed to rest. It was hard to keep up with him. He smiled and told her to lie down and take a nap. Her ravens gathered round her fluttering and flapping their wings, stirring up the air as she began to fall asleep. Suddenly, her body felt heavy. She heard a splash and she realized she was in the river!

"You are safe, do not worry," she heard a soothing voice say. It was the water. She began to feel warm and comforted as the water swirled around her as if wrapping her in its arms. Despite being submerged in the crystal-clear river she noticed she could breathe easily.

Bear was next to her singing his medicine songs. She felt his necklace of feathers and beads near her heart. She was relieved to know he was with her.

'Bear sang his medicine song into her heart.'

Her ravens dove in and out of the water. They were talking fast about how this was more than just a river. The girl with the ravens felt that she was deep in the body of the water. She began hearing a soft lullaby over Bear's medicine song. It was a lullaby she remembered hearing as a child. The music began to pierce her whole body like a bright light piercing dense matter.

Bear's voice came through telling her to hold on, so she squeezed his paw tightly as the water swirled around them creating a huge tunnel. She saw the black feathers of her ravens glistening in the water as they rushed through the tunnel to the other end.

"We are almost there!" cackled one of her ravens on top of her head. The spiraling water catapulted them like comets into the Universe. Bear helped her to her feet. Remarkably, she was not wet. How can this be she thought to herself?

Bear smiled having heard her thought, "The water is alive and provides life for everyone in the Universe. It is intelligent, it hears you, heals you and transports you."

A dense forest and long grass was growing exactly where they were standing, "Where are we?"

Bear said, "We have traveled across the galaxy to another world."

Then her ravens gathered around her protectively, "Someone is coming," they squawked.

Through the wooded landscape she saw a man moving towards her who traveled in the body of a serpent. At first, she did not recognize him but then as he approached the serpent god became clearer and clearer. The girl with many ravens blinked back tears that were now streaming down her face. This was someone she hadn't seen since she was a child.

"How is it you are here?"

The serpent god smiled, "The water has brought you to my home so that I could give you a gift."

The girl with many ravens nodded her head in reverence to him. "I am honored to see you."

The serpent god told her, "I came to you when you were a child. You have always been a part of the water and its medicine. I used to sing you a song and weave its magical melody into your hair to teach you about the river. Do you remember finding small iridescent stones by the water?"

With surprise she said, "Yes, I do remember finding those on the river bank, but I did not realize they were from you."

The serpent god replied, "These stones were symbolic of the energy created by the sound of my song and the power of the river. You have the sight and the connection that is needed to care for the water."

"But what can I do?"

He placed an iridescent stone like the ones she used to find on the bank of the river in her hand and said, "You are like a star that shines bright while living on Earth. This stone gives you passage into my realm because you are now a protector of the water. I am always here to help you."

She looked over at Bear and he was smiling.

The serpent god went on, "You must remember the power of the water is ever present and your words, actions and song have a great effect on it. Do not underestimate your abilities to call upon the water to guide you. Water is for all life in the Universe; it not only communicates with us but is a conduit for travel."

The girl with many ravens held the stone tight in her hand and her memories of the many times she spent at the river's edge flooded her mind.

The serpent god smiled at the girl and said, "Put the stone in your pocket for safe keeping."

They were the last words she heard him say. Then the nearby river rose around them swirling. The ravens croaked with delight, the wind shifted, and the water became a spiraling tunnel again.

She woke on the bank of the river. Bear was by her side sleeping soundly. Forming a protective circle around them were the ravens keeping watch. She sat up, blinked at the bright sunlight.

Bear sat up, "Who is hungry?"

The ravens cried, "We are, we are."

The girl slipped the stone out of her pocket and looked at it once again. A bright light radiated from within it. She smiled.

Bear noticed the light in her hand and said, "There is so much to be grateful for here on Earth. I am glad the water took us where we needed to go."

She thanked Bear for his medicine and their journey.

"Without your knowledge, I would still be sitting by the river's edge," the girl said.

The ravens made clicking sounds and then they broke into a roar of laughter. "We would still be sitting here too," they cried!

Bear's nose sniffed the air. "I smell breakfast, let's go!"

The River's Edge is about the importance of water and its spiritual component that we interact with daily. Water covers 71% of the Earth's surface and it goes without saying that without it humans and life on Earth would perish. What we rarely consider though is how spiritually connected we are to it and it is vital that humans develop a deeper understanding of this powerful element. In understanding our spiritual connection to water, we should probably remember that there is only a small amount of fresh water on the Earth's surface – 0.3%. We live under the illusion that there is plenty of water available since so much of the Earth's surface is covered with it, but perhaps we are unaware of how precious our fresh water is. What can we do spiritually as humans to better our relationship to water? As a healer, I think it's important to understand the water in our bodies first. The human brain is 73% water, the lungs 83%, and our skin is 64% water. When we realize how water in our body is connected with all the water of the Earth we begin to see the spiritual importance of this element.

For centuries, indigenous peoples of all nations have practiced ceremonies celebrating the universal relationship we humans have with this sacred element. We have prayed to the water, and to the deity who governs it, asking for healing, safe travels and rain. Water's role in the food chain is essential and probably the most important connection we have to the element. For thousands of years, ancient peoples of all cultures designed ceremonies around the world to bring rain so that crops may grow, and the people survive. In fact, in my own Hopi culture water is so revered that before the people begin to put a ceremony together there must be the intention of a pure heart and mind to bring about the fruition of rainfall. When the hearts and minds of people are not aligned then they will often bring nothing but wind. This is a good reminder of how mindful we all need to be in our spiritual practice.

We take water for granted forgetting the sacred energy it carries. It may start in the ocean and end up in the river and rain upon the ground that ends up in the reservoir and pours out your faucet and ultimately becomes a part of you. Just like the girl with many ravens who becomes a part of the water and the water becomes a part of her – water is in everything and water is a part of everything. If we understand the many sacred passages water makes we might better care for it, our bodies and the planet.

Japanese author Masaru Emoto has done extensive research on the relationship between the human consciousness and the molecular structure of water, and how one affects the other. He has shown that positive vibrations and emotional energies can influence water molecules. His experiments have also shown that prayer and visualization can have positive effects on polluted water. When water is exposed to beautiful music, pictures or positive spoken words and then frozen, the resulting crystals studied through microscopic photography resulted in stunning formations. When a negative approach was taken the crystals were malformed. Emoto believed water was the blueprint for our reality.

Our ancestors understood well what Emoto wanted us to remember – water is life. The serpent god gave the girl with many ravens an iridescent stone as a reminder that she was a guardian for this sacred water. We are all caregivers of planet Earth, this is our mission from the beginning of time until now. Without each one of us taking a stand to protect the fresh water that is available to us we will only have ourselves to blame if fresh water sources disappear. We live in a time in which we can no longer remain complacent. Our spiritual connection to water is more powerful than people truly understand. We can contribute spiritually to care for the water by simply praying over it when we take a bath or a shower or use an irrigation system. Before we drink a glass of water we can ask for healing and protection and we might even consider that when we listen to music we are activating the water in our body. Do not miss the opportunity to adjust your internal and external water to a higher frequency.

'She rose out of the meadow powerful
and enormous.'

15

Earth Spirit

Bear sat in the grass in the middle of a meadow that was surrounded by forest. He saw Raven flying overhead and called out to him. Raven swooped down and landed near Bear. "What's up?"

Bear said, "I am feeling the world is not right. I have bad dreams at night of the land and all life being destroyed. I know in my heart there is a sickness that is spreading."

Raven croaked, "The illness is greed. Too bad, humans can't see the future."

Bear reached into his bag and brought out his drum. He told Raven he was going to sing a song for the Earth. As he sang, the animals from the forest came to the meadow. They gathered around Bear to listen.

All at once Raven saw the ground they were standing on beginning to move. He yelled out to the animals gathered around Bear, "Get back! Get back!"

The animals scattered almost toppling Bear in their rush.

From the center of the meadow a cloud of dust and smoke rose out of the ground. The Earth shook, and the ground cracked open. The Spirit of the Earth, powerful and enormous, was rising up out of the land before them. Bear looked up in awe as she continued to rise above them. She was taller than the trees. There was silence. The astonished animals stared at the enormous spirit before them.

She spoke. Her voice was like honey, warm and deep. "Who called me?" she asked.

"I did," said Bear. "I called you with my song."

Raven cackled. "Now you're in trouble!"

Bear shushed him.

"Why have you summoned me?"

"I wanted to ask you what can be done for all of the harm that takes place on the Earth."

The enormous Spirit gravely lowered her eyes and said, "There is nothing you can do. This is a part of my purpose. I provide a place for all life to live and I care for everyone as my children. Would you discard or throw away your child?"

Bear and Raven shook their heads, no.

"My task is to help all life learn what is necessary in the development of the Universe. This is but one stop for all of you. You may come back to me in multiple lives but ultimately you will go on and develop new planets in the Universe."

Raven chimed in, "We blew it, I knew it, we blew it!" He was cackling and shaking his head.

Suddenly the air got still again. Her voice boomed from her body. "Do not presume you have failed. The question stands: have you understood your lesson? Know this, I need many repairs. My blood, bones and organs have been harvested from my body. My body, like the body of many humans, is surviving under duress. I understand how the human desire to live free, includes having more. The animal kingdom is the only life form living without greed. You might beg to differ with the behavior of squirrels, but they are more absent-minded than greedy. Humans cannot get past their desire for more. They are wounded at birth because of their separation from Creator. I do my best to mother them and love them with nature."

She looked away, "Even now they reject me and continue to deny my very existence by paving over my skin and taking my blood."

Bear asked, "What can we do?"

"Nothing. I have been in this celestial body for billions of years. My life span is much longer than yours. I too will find a new body when it is my time to cross over. My celestial soul has a different calling and requires me to be unconditional as I play a direct role in karma. The karma incurred in each life happens on my soil, but I do not create karma in the ways of humans. My soul is of a much higher consciousness. The planets are related to Creator. We are celestial beings. Our vibration is even higher than that of the demi gods."

Raven made a gurgling sound and said, "What about the water?"

"There will always be water, but most of it is polluted. That will not change until the planet is cleansed. I experience cleansing every three hundred thousand years. This helps me regulate my body. I am not that different from any species. I need nourishment, love and shelter too."

She smiled at the animals who were listening intently. Then she laughed a loud roaring laugh. She said, "There is nothing to worry about. You are all having a physical experience on a planet that displays much aggression, conflict and disruption. To not reflect those things back to your mother is a tall order. The animal kingdom stays true to form because they live more in the natural world. Humans are evolving and try to resist the urge to be aggressive and create conflicts. For centuries, they have given in to these energies that surround my body. This evolution of the human species is why they came here to begin with. They wanted to be challenged and placed on a planet that could force them to grow. There is a much bigger picture that is hard to see when you are living on my surface. Earth's gravity and atmosphere demands a great deal of energy from all life. No one is to blame for the nature of my turbulence. There is only the experience of tornados, hurricanes, flooding, fires, earthquakes and volcanic eruptions."

She looked out at the animals as she crossed her hand over them. "You incur my life path. Pick another planet, there will be another path to follow."

Bear noticed the ground starting to move again. He quickly said, "Thank you, Goddess, we are your humble servants."

"You are always under my watchful eye, Bear. You too, Raven."

The ground opened up once again and the Earth Spirit disappeared. The animals scattered to the four directions taking her teachings back to their families.

Bear looked at Raven, "Now I know why I have not been feeling right. The world is on end. I must do something to help," he said.

Raven cocked his head sideways, "What are you going to do?"

"I am going to get my drum and sing the planet back to health!"

Raven ruffled his feathers, "I will find something to eat."

Bear shrugged his shoulders at Raven. He pulled his drum out of his bag and started to sing a song taught to him by his mother. It was a healing song. The wind picked up. The trees responded. The grass and plants lifted toward the sun swaying in the wind. Raven flew high overhead. He could hear Bear's song echoing through the valley. Bear kept singing all through the night and into the morning. Animals that lived nearby brought him food. Day after day he sang.

Then on the fourth day the ground around him shook and once again the Earth Spirit rose from below.

"Bear you sang until your voice has gone. I am in gratitude for your song and the prayer that goes with it. I feel the healing in my body. This is powerful medicine that you have. This is the way things will change. It is your belief that I can heal. That belief gives way to a magic that has been long gone. You have brought this magic back to the Earth. Thank you, Bear, for your song."

He sat there, exhausted and bowed his head.
Once more the Earth Spirit vanished.
Bear laid down, resting his eyes. When he woke up, it was the
next day. The meadow was bright. All the birds sang. The water
in the creek ran clear and Raven danced in the wind.

Today, many humans appear to have little faith, with the focus on technology and a much faster pace. Hundreds of years ago faith was all humans had, there was no television or cell phones to distract an essential human experience. Faith is something that comes in and out of fashion based on societal beliefs. We witness Bear delving deep into his faith believing that he could help the Earth Spirit. In the Lakota/Sioux tradition a man will participate in a sun dance pierced to a tree and praying for his life and his family. No food or water is allowed – only faith. Just like crawling into a sweat lodge, it is the mother's womb, dark and warm and requiring faith. As each stone is brought in one at a time and water blesses them, we learn to surrender to having faith, both from the heat and the ceremony.

These types of ceremonies and rituals were more common in the ancient past because people understood that everything has spirit. Just like Bear singing the song to the Earth, his voice carries a vibration that's intent is pure. Sound is a powerful healing tool that each person has access to. Along with sound comes vibration.

Since the time of Atlantis, all life lived in the fourth dimension. As a species we have been content living lifetime after lifetime in the same frequency. When the Mayan calendar ended, we moved into the fifth dimension. This is not an everyday occurrence. This is considered a major shift in our understanding of all things on Earth and beyond the pressure of what has been (the history of the first four dimensions) is now pushing to be released; consequently humanity is struggling to adjust to this higher frequency. Bear and Raven remind us of our connection to the Earth and this is where we should keep our focus. As the fifth dimension continues to unfold for centuries to come we are the pioneers of this new frequency. Staying focused on our connection to Earth will help us to integrate such a major shift.

The fifth dimension is like a train station. It is not a place to stop and settle but rather determine where we will go next. The fifth dimension is gathering the energy of what has been created by the human race. This incredible pressure is pushing for the sixth and seventh dimensions to be released. At the end of the Mayan calendar the fourth dimension came to a close and we started moving faster through the various dimensions. It can be hard to maintain our individual energy as we all struggle to find balance in a higher frequency.

The Earth Spirit is contending with the higher vibration of the new dimension and the energy of the galaxy. She must shift into this higher frequency as all who live upon her must. Her transition may be a bit bumpy like ours. Mankind feels the Earth's energy and the need for it to release in the form of volcanic eruptions, hurricanes, earthquakes and tornadoes.

Bear's concern that something isn't right and that things are out of balance is something many of us are aware of. But he learns that when problems are bigger than ourselves we can rely on our faith, and trust in Creator and the Goddess or Earth – that it is all unfolding as it should. The Earth Spirit makes it clear to Bear that we will go through what we go through living on her body and making this transition at this time. She reminds Bear that there is nothing that he can do to control any of this, instead he must submit to it along with her. There is a much bigger force at play in the Universe. This is the path that he has chosen. Learning to trust is mapped out in our early childhood development. A new born baby learns trust through their parents. This organic process sets the stage for trusting our environment as adults. The Earth's natural environment lends to a continual lesson on trust. Understanding the true nature of this planet helps us to love her unconditionally and care for her, for without her we have nothing.

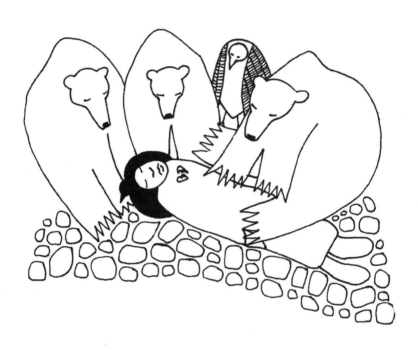

'The healers mended her broken heart as vulture
watched, waiting for the outcome.'

16

Mending a Broken Heart

She had a broken heart. Her love for a man had clouded her judgment and she fell off the cliff, plummeting to the ground below. The medicine bears were busy holding their monthly council meeting nearby and saw a young woman falling from the sky. Vulture appeared and said, "Do you want me to go get her?"

The bears replied, "Yes, please do and bring her to us."

Vulture thought there might be a meal in this for him, so he was eager to get the girl. Luckily, she had landed in the soft moss on the forest floor. She sat up looking bewildered.

Vulture said, "You are hurt, let me take you to some healers."

The young woman looked at Vulture and said, "I will not go with you! I have a broken heart and I just fell off that cliff, besides I don't know you."

Vulture put on his best friendly face, "Ah, but I know you."

She looked at him and blinked. Then she remembered seeing him recently. He was feasting voraciously on something in the middle of the forest. "Oh! I do remember you. You were at the feast in the forest." She realized the vulture was looking at her in the most peculiar way.

Not wanting to be lunch, she got up quickly and began to walk away, but again she fell. Her legs were wobbly and could not hold her. She felt her spirit rise up as if it meant to leave her body, but her broken heart would not allow it.

Vulture returned to the bears. He told them he needed help with the young woman. By the time they reached her the bears could see that her desire to live was leaving her body. It was like a wisp of smoke rising up out of her heart. Together, they carried the young woman to their home and placed her body on the healing stones. The bears listened as the stones told them her story of how a young man she loved more than life itself had left her for another. The stones told the bears that her love for this man was all consuming and that it caused her to lose herself.

The bears went to work on mending her heart. They wrapped cedar around her ankles and wrists to bring her back into this world. She stirred and looked up to see the medicine bears looking back at her. Vulture was watching over their shoulders now feeling pity for the young woman after hearing her story. One bear said, "We have mended your heart and brought you back into this world. You will stay with us until you are completely healed."

She looked at the bear and said, "My heart no longer hurts, and I feel like myself again. What happened to me?"

"You were overtaken by your desire to be loved and gave so much of yourself that you almost disappeared. In fact, we watched you lose your desire to live. You must remember you have a magnificent heart. Within you is the little girl who tries hard to gain validation and love from others. If you give that immense love to yourself first you will succeed in loving others without experiencing a broken heart. Our heart breaks because when we give our love we also have expectations. It takes time to learn unconditional love for we must first start by loving ourselves.

She felt her heart stir with a truth that made sense beyond words. As she lay there on the healing stones she noticed her hands tingling and her feet warm. The bears looked at one another and asked, "Are you ready?"

"Yes," she replied. Now she felt a pressure in her spine.

The raven on top of her head cried out, "Now you change yourself!"

She sat up and spat out a feather that had stuck to her tongue.

She had a beak, and black feathers now adorned her body. She squawked and whispered, "Excuse me."

The raven that was once on her head, now stood next to her and smiled. "I am so happy to have you back. I have waited for this day since you were born."

"What happened?" she squawked.

The bears gathered and explained to her that she had returned to her original raven form. They had turned her into a human, so she could learn how to manage her abilities and heal from the death of her parents. The bears had found her lost and frightened in the woods when she was just a small raven.

"We took you in and cared for you. We could see your wounded heart and at the same time a very powerful magic inside of you. As you grew we knew there was no way you could wield this power unless you found healing."

She looked at them and cried, "Why didn't you ask me?"

The bears lowered their eyes and said, "We did ask you, but as a young raven you were strong willed and defiant, and you told us you didn't need our help." The bears went on to say, "It was your heart that brought you back to us. You have learned now how powerful the energy of love is and that it can bring a person to total destruction if it is not managed with care and guidance. Love is something we all have and share. It is something we must give to ourselves, that wee little bird inside, so we can wield the gifts we are born with."

The raven looked at the bears and thanked them for helping her. She was happy to return to her natural state. She looked over at the other raven who had sat on her head so diligently protecting her all these years and said to him, "Are you ready?"

They took flight and circled the bears squawking and cackling. Vulture grinned and said, "Who's hungry?"

The bears laughed and made their way to the feast that was taking place in the middle of the forest.

When we can learn to love all parts of ourselves including our emotional wounds and undesirable personality traits we learn a great lesson about the heart. As the young woman experienced in the story, her obsession with her lover causes her to lose sight of herself. It takes deep transformation for her to come back to her true self. There are different kinds of love. When we are in obsessive love, we ultimately suffer. All-consuming love has within it an expectation that 'the other' or the 'loved' will do something or be something that we want. And when that doesn't happen we are heartbroken. In the case of the young woman she is left by her lover – the man she has invested her heart in. Many people have experienced the loss of a partner, and it can feel as if a part of their own soul has left them. This kind of heartbreak can be paralyzing and prevent us from moving on and finding a new happiness. When we love from a healthy perspective we start first with ourselves. This way we can address and process our emotions with a better understanding of how to love and have compassion for ourselves. It is from this place that our compassion expands and reaches others.

The bears' compassion for the young woman reminds us that there are healers in the world that can help us along our way. The vulture represents the hunger for love that humanity feels, just like his desperation to have another meal that will satisfy the emptiness inside. The ravens are curious, intelligent and often strong willed with a mind of their own. All of these characters represent those parts of ourselves that want to be loved, cherished and respected. The stones represent the intelligence of the Earth and they provide information to the bears during the young woman's healing. This indicates that there is spirit in all things and that that spirit has intelligence. In my native culture we believe that spirit resides in everything from the stones to the plants and trees and the stars above.

Rarely do we think about love in terms of having boundaries. We usually think about love as a riot in the heart creating a blissful endless experience. In the story of this young woman we learn that she did not understand that giving of herself and her love to such an extreme would render her helpless. When we grow up in a dysfunctional family it is often accompanied by co-dependency. Co-dependency focuses on the needs of others and blurs the lines of healthy boundaries. When we address our own co-dependent behavior we can create healthy boundaries. These healthy boundaries are not necessarily something we are born with, they are learned. The best way to create healthy boundaries is to stay aware of your feelings and to make sure you do not take on another person's emotions. Unconditional love is loving at the deepest level of your being. Few of us ever get there because love is often interpreted through the lens of our emotional wounds. We have to become the observer, grounded and centered within our own experience; acknowledging the feelings of others but not taking them on board, to have the ability to love unconditionally. The spiritual lesson of "mending a broken heart" first and foremost is that it is about karma. You absolutely have had past lives with the person who broke your heart. In fact, we share karma with everyone we come into contact with. Lovers and important relationships come into our lives to clear karma and to reflect back to us our emotional wounds. At times broken hearts can push us to the point of spiritual upheaval. This spiritual crisis can be the key to our relationship with Creator. Once we have healed the core wound of separation from source we will no longer experience a broken heart.

17

Warriors of the Earth

Long ago there was a group of women who knew the old ways of Earth Medicine. They were happy living their lives next to the Earth, gathering her plants and singing her songs. They lived in a small village next to the sea. They would plant their gardens according to the moon and use the stars to navigate their lives. They each held a position that was specific to the medicine of the Earth. One woman was in charge of the night and dreamed her dreams for the entire village. Another was in charge of the daylight and kept a candle burning to make sure the sun could see her prayer, and yet another was in charge of the plants. Other women held positions for the wood, songs, animals, wind and fire.

The women prayed to the one who ruled the sea. They asked him if he would grant them help with their magic. He said, "Yes." They were excited and planned for a ceremony, which would be held the next night. The moon shone bright and smiled down upon them. The ancient God from the sea came out of the water and stood near the circle of women. They all felt his energy and the Ravens on their heads stirred.

The women said they wanted to do good things for the people and the Earth. The Sea God smiled and said, "You are doing good things for the people and the Goddess. Why do you need more power for your magic?"

The woman in charge of all of the songs spoke first. "We want to heal people all over the world and help them to honor the Earth and her medicine."

~

'They were women, warriors in another time.
They dedicated their love to the Earth.
They were somewhere between this world and the next.'

The Sea God replied, "There is a place I can take you to where you will be very helpful to all of humanity."

He had the women climb into a boat. The bright moonlight shone upon the water as the God of the Sea moved the ocean this way and that, creating small waves that carried the boat to a place the women did not recognize.

The dreamer asked, "Where are we? I have seen this place in my dreams."

He replied, "You are between worlds!"

The blue water turned green, then red, silver and gold. The sky merged with the sea and the women did not know if up was down or down was up. They felt disoriented and a bit frightened in their boat.

The Sea God explained that what they were asking for required them to be much stronger, able to face whatever was put before them. He went on to tell them they were warriors of the light. The women could see energy swirling around each of them merging their bodies with the ocean and the sky.

The Sea God said, "It is done."

All of a sudden, the Ravens on top of their heads started squawking and croaking, "Look over there!"

The women all looked across the water toward the landscape. They could see a dock and village that looked like their own. The boat glided to the dock. They all came to shore.

The Ravens were talking amongst themselves saying this was the land between worlds. The Ravens said, "We have not been here for a long, long time."

The Sea God smiled and said, "You will find this village exactly as your own and your homes in place. By coming here, you have chosen to be in service to all of humanity."

The woman who tends to the plants said, "How will we know that what we are doing is helping everyone if we are here between worlds?"

The Sea God replied, "You will have to trust your efforts and be true to the Goddess and Creator. You are still connected to Earth. You are simply living with a different understanding. Your lives are dedicated to being in service and by remaining here you can help without distraction."

They all gathered up their things and walked into the village. They looked behind to see the Sea God moving across the water.

They discovered that their homes were still there, and the garden planted exactly as they had left it. In fact, all of the people in the village were exactly the same. The woman in charge of the daylight asked, "How can this be? Are we really between worlds?"

The Raven on her head said, "Yes of course, this is real, and you are back home where you started. Only now you have a new understanding of reality. When you commit to being in service to the Earth and helping all who live upon her body, doors open to other realities. You are now living in a space somewhere between this world and the next. There is no difference between where you came from and where you are now but at the same time everything has changed."

The women smiled as they walked back to their homes. Now they truly understood what it was that they had asked of the Sea God — having power was a great responsibility. To wield such power, one must live between worlds, dedicated to being in service.

In Norse mythology Jormungand is a sea-serpent, referred to as the Midgard Serpent in old Norse texts. He's one of the three children of Loki and the giantess Angrboða. Jormungand was cast into the ocean and grew so large his body circles all of Midgard, which is the visible world in the nine realms. Many cultures of the past recognize this ancient protector of the water. My father, who was a Norwegian raised me to believe in the importance of our relationship to water. Just like the people of the ancient past I was taught that the water was governed by a powerful spirit and that spirit took the form of a serpent. Moreover, I was named for the water in my Hopi culture which means I am forever "in service" to the water.

What does it mean to be "in service"? We are living in a time consumed with technology and easy access to answers that we can Google and find on our phones. The Earth is a living being just as we are. She relies on her inhabitants to live according to the natural laws. This means living in sync with the cycle of life, caring for the surface of the planet as well as deep underground as if it were our own body. Being "in service" means turning our lives over to Creator and the Earth to serve humanity, the planet and all living upon her.

To be a "warrior" of the Earth means that you are not only in service but that you are committed to fighting for her preservation. This does not mean through violence. This means you are a "spiritual warrior", someone willing to commit themselves spiritually to this planet. The air, water, land and all-natural resources need our protection. Your involvement through your spiritual practice helps the Earth. She is much bigger than all of us. She is a Goddess with a much longer life span than the human experience. Her status in the Universe, like all planets, is similar to the demi gods that I describe in my book, *Spirit Traveler*. They have a different soul cycle to humans.

Now that we are in the Fifth Dimension we are watching the Earth transform and many people are feeling its effects. The Earth is getting ready to make her own evolutionary jump and the evidence is all around us as lands shift, the ice age approaches and volcanos release built up pressure. Climatologists tell us that the Earth warms before an Ice Age. This allows certain parts of the Earth to heal from over use and depletion of natural resources. We are not the first phase of humanity to end with Earth shifts and climate change. Like the ancient civilizations of Atlantis and Lumeria, during which extreme geological shifts on Earth reduced human population, we can expect the same in our times. This will help us in the long run to find balance once again on her surface.

Being a "spiritual warrior" is not an easy task. Your integrity must be high and your ego in such a state of balance that you are okay having nothing, being nothing and not expecting anything. Sit in meditation and allow yourself to feel those feelings. If your fear comes up, observe it. Feel it and release it into the Earth. If you feel combative and want to hang on to your title or position in life, then you know your ego remains invested in what you are doing. Let it go. When we truly embrace that we are infinite souls having a human experience, then our ability to dedicate ourselves to a life of service as a spiritual warrior is possible.

Make your daily practice one of forgiveness of yourself and others.

Align your spiritual practice with Creator and the Earth.

Tell your story to the Earth, sharing your feelings with her as you would another person.

Surrender your attachment to things, people and titles. Live in a state of nothingness so you can truly experience everything.

Understand there are many realities and where we put our focus, energetically, is where we will be manifesting.

'I am afraid for my child. I do not know
what will happen and I fear there will be no world left
for her to grow up in.'

18

The Next Seven Generations

Raven flew across the top ridge. Beneath him at the edge of the forest he saw a woman carrying a baby. He swooped down and squawked, "Where are you going?"

He landed on a nearby branch of a cedar tree and watched her. She looked up at Raven and he saw she had tears in her eyes. The woman shouted, "Go away Raven!" The woman sat down on the bare ground holding her baby, who she had named Sara, in her arms. She began sobbing uncontrollably. Raven became concerned. He took off to find Bear.

"Bear Bear!" he croaked and cackled outside Bear's cave. From within he heard a low grumble and moments later a sleepy looking Bear emerged wrapped in a blanket. "What is wrong, Raven?"

"There is a woman with a child in the forest, she is crying. You had better go to help her."

Bear dropped the blanket and began running. Raven sighed, then squawked after Bear, "What would Bear do without me?" And he flew inside the Bear's cave and grabbed the Bear's medicine bag. Then he took off after Bear. By the time Bear reached the woman he had transformed into a man. He didn't want to scare her. The young woman saw the man approaching and jumped to her feet.

"Don't worry I am here to help you," he said. "Raven told me you were in trouble." The woman shot Raven a nasty look. "I told you to go away," she said to Raven. "I will be fine. Go away."

Bear sat down. He scratched behind his ear and then broke into a smile as he remembered it was a human ear and his vigorous scratching and long nails had dug deep into the skin. He was puzzled by the woman's reaction.

The woman spoke, "I heard there was a medicine man in this forest, but I can't find him."

Bear, who had now transformed fully into a man, sat up straight and said, "But you have found him, I am him and he is me!"

Raven made a scoffing sound and rolled his eyes. Then the baby started to cry. Her mother began to rock her trying to soothe the infant. "You don't look like a medicine man." the woman said to him. "Where are your braids and moccasins?"

The medicine man looked down. He realized he was dressed in lightweight pants and a tee shirt with no shoes, just bare feet! His hair flowed wild down his back. He looked at Raven and rolled his eyes.

"Well I am a medicine man. So, what can I help you with?"

The woman took a deep breath and said, "I am Atla and I am afraid for my baby, Sara. What is this Earth coming to? I'm afraid for my child's future and that there will be no world left for Sara to grow up in."

The medicine man sat down again. He reached into his medicine bag and took out a rattle. He began to sing a medicine song. The medicine man's smooth voice worked immediately, and baby Sara fell asleep. He began to doctor the distressed woman who rocked to the steady sound of the medicine man's rattle. A dense mist descended from the trees and shapes began to take form around her. She recognized the six ghostly figures that stood before her as her maternal ancestors.

"Atla! Atla!" one of the women called out.

"I am right here mama." Her mother, Rose stood before her and in the vision Atla could see herself as a child in her mother's arms. Rose was hugging her tightly and telling her with a calm reassuring voice that the world would still be there in the morning when she wakes up.

The medicine man kept singing.

Next, she saw a vision of her Grandmother and her mother, Rose as a little girl. Her Grandmother was wearing the same clothes she remembered her in – a warm wool sweater over a blue dress with giant pockets filled with peppermint Lifesavers. This time her mother turned to her Grandmother, who was named Astrild, after the goddess of love, and said, "I am so worried about our future." The Grandmother hugged Rose and said, "There is always a new day."

As that vision faded, Atla held her baby tight. The next vision was of her Great Grandmother, named Kara. She was a tiny woman with thick black hair neatly woven in braid down her back. She was wise and very powerful. Kara was calling out to her daughter, Astrild who came running to her as a small child crying and telling her she was scared. The Great Grandmother held her Astrild tight and said, "Nothing can harm you, for you are always protected by Creator."

Atla smiled as she recognized her Great Grandmother's words. There was another shift and the vision changed once again. The woman who stood before her was her Great, Great Grandmother named Evelyn who had long dark hair and traditional clothing. She gazed at her daughter, Kara who looked despondent and was clearly distressed, "The white man has waged war against us. We have been separated and forced to move from our homes. Our family members have been killed."

Great, Great Grandmother, Evelyn reached her hand through the veil and touched the forehead of Atla. She smiled and nodded to the medicine man and then she said, "No matter how much fear there is, it all boils down to faith. You must believe Creator will guide and help you."

Her Great, Great, Great Grandmother, Saga entered the vision and looked right at Atla and said, "Never doubt the strength of your mother, the Earth. She has taken care of us through wars, destruction and disease. We are strong because we trust Creator will take care of us. The next seven generations will survive if you teach your children humility, forgiveness and to love everyone equally."

The baby, Sara was awake now and staring at the vision of her ancestors. She gurgled and smiled as her many grandmothers from the past gave her a pat and a wink and the vision faded.

The medicine man said, "Your family is strong, and you have many ancestors watching over you."

Atla replied, "Thank you. I know you have revealed what I needed to hear and see."

Bear helped her to her feet. She handed the baby to him. He rubbed some medicine on the baby's head and spoke a blessing in his native tongue.

They walked to the edge of the forest and parted ways. She turned around to wave but only saw a bear lumbering off into the woods. Raven flew overhead, cackling, "Goodbye, Goodbye."

Within every era there are those who believe that their generation's time on Earth will be the last. Doomsday is upon us and those believers even have a clock that tells us how close we are to total destruction. If we listen to those who predict Armageddon, we are left with only a choice to live in constant fear. Trusting in something greater than ourselves has been the struggle of humanity since the beginning of our Earth time. We have doubted Creator through many historic events. For example, in my book, *Spirit Traveler*, I explain how the people of Stonehenge were so distraught their gods were no longer appearing to them that when a high priestess would die they would bury them next to the monument in hopes they could bring the gods back. Those burial mounds still stand today and have many archaeologists scratching heads.

Humans have found their faith tested during periods of famine, disease pandemics and world war. No matter how many millions have perished there are always those who survive. With each generation the fear of being one of those who does not survive leads to anxiety about death. Having faith that there is something beyond physical death is the big question and doubt all humans experience. The struggle to come to terms with the idea of death and what lies beyond it is one that humans will face into perpetuity.

On a more universal scale the survival of this planet is as fragile as our own existence. We do not necessarily see the grand scope of the Earth's history because it spans millions of years. We are a part of her journey and she is part of ours.

What we learn from each grandmother in the story of *The Next Seven Generations* is that no matter what the circumstances or situation at hand we must have faith. I remember my mother comforting me as a child when I asked what would happen to the Earth. She told me not to worry and said that when she was a child people thought the world would end with World War Two. She told me that according to the news, the world was supposed to end every day! We have a choice. We can either worry ourselves silly or have faith in our Creator. The Earth certainly has patience and offers us everything that we need. It is up to us to fulfill our purpose as the caretakers of this planet and trust in a higher power.

Conclusion

I have spent 36 years as a healer working with people from all walks of life and for most of that time the message I have been trying to communicate is one of our connectivity to the Earth and our spiritual evolutionary process; in other words, explaining why we are here. Our karma is the thread that ties all of our lives and this lifetime together. And for me my karmic history is deeply tied to the Norse gods and my Hopi culture.

My own relationship to Raven and Bear is not only expressed through my artwork but alive as a daily experience that inspired me to write these stories – Raven and Bear have been constant companions throughout my life. But it may surprise the reader to learn that I wasn't always aware of the Norwegian influence that connected me to Raven and Bear. Years ago, when my artwork was hanging in a gallery for purchase a Norwegian man, who was an art collector, pointed out that by painting Raven and Bear I was in fact painting Norse lore, part of my heritage. My life journey has led me to a place of storytelling because I find it connects to the heart and soul of the reader. Storytelling has a unique way of engaging the inner child in all of us.

I have always understood that when we look to nature for our teachings we can begin to experience a whole new reality. Earth Medicine is the spiritual aspect of nature and our experience of it. These stories open a doorway for understanding how powerful Earth Medicine really is. It is like a ray of sunshine. It fills us, altering our understanding and expanding our consciousness into the universe. Everything is alive with its own spiritual component even the elements fire, water, wind and earth hold a much higher frequency. In *Dancing with Raven and Bear*, these elemental deities are teachers to Raven and Bear and all who come into contact with them. As humans it is not until we awaken to the complexity of Earth that we truly understand this. The myths and stories of the ancient people of Scandinavia and the indigenous people of North America all have something in common in that they recognize the spirit in all things. Scandinavian myths refer to the elements like the North Wind as having a voice and spirit in the same way that my own Hopi culture believes the wind is powerful and lives between two rocks.

Many things that the ancient people understood they also feared. The ancient stories told in Norse mythology often identify the mountains, sea and forest as dark and strange places where one might encounter undesirable energies. These myths often included evil spirits and monsters that were woven into tales to protect the people from going to certain areas or falling prey to the unknown. In our modern world we still name the elements and natural phenomenon, such as hurricanes. While naming helps the scientists to identify them, in the popular psyche, naming hurricanes like Andrew, Katrina and Harvey also gives them a larger than life energy leaving people in fear of something we cannot control.

Feeling secure and safe is the opposite of fear. Humans measure all emotions in duality: good/bad, love/hate, right/wrong. It is through this external measuring system that humans literally hook up their emotional energy with other humans. You might ask what's wrong with someone connecting with my love, my joy and my happiness? There is nothing wrong with it, except that when we understand how karma works, we will understand that engaging our energy in dualism continues to create more karma. In each lifetime it is our responsibility to be clearing our karma not creating more. In *Dancing with Raven and Bear* duality is constant but so is the goal of becoming aware and ultimately an observer of duality.

The duality exists in many forms in myths and stories of my heritage – most commonly it can be found in tales of the underworld and overworld. This duality exists in Hopi culture. While the Kachinas or mythical deities visit the people during the spring and summer months, it is in fact wintertime and quiet in the underworld. And when it is winter here on Earth the Kachinas are busy with ceremonies and helping the people in the underworld. In Hopi culture the underworld is considered the spirit world. The same concept exists in Norse mythology in the stories of Odin and the nine realms.

Many of the stories I tell in *Dancing with Raven and Bear* have characters that shape-shift. In Norse mythology, Odin's adopted son Loki is a shape-shifter who takes the form of his father, Thor and others to manipulate and control what he fears will never be his, Asgard (the home of Odin). He is a coyote, or trickster who has several emotional wounds of separation and betrayal which constantly lead him down a menacing path. Shape-shifters in today's world are considered shamans or medicine men and women who take the form of an animal to observe a situation or gather information. This is not always done with integrity and respect as I explain in some of the stories about Bear. Bear lives by the rule of being in service and never misuses his power. Mankind has misused power for centuries and those who have the ability to shape shift walk a dangerous road, always tempted to misuse their power.

When we imagine ourselves as a bear, fox or hawk we might feel the inner stirring of our own animal totem. I believe each person has seven animals that relate and live within their seven chakras. In my stories, people are animals and animals are people. When I work with clients I often guide them to their own personal totem. These animals are the magic that is within each one of us. Our outer pets or wildlife that we see in the woods or fields reflect those inner helpers. There is often meaning to seeing a deer, fox or hawk while driving home. That animal might have a message for you that is read through the direction it travels, whether it is standing still or moving and what is happening at the time you see it. If what you saw was a shape-shifter you will notice an odd behavior from the animal. Most shifters are not adept to the form they have taken. It is common for the animal that appears to be one that is found in your totem. The magic that is derived from seeing one of your own totem animals can be uplifting and life affirming. I have long believed that animals are the healers of this planet.

Sometimes, we might dream about a pet or an animal or it might appear to us during the day bringing a message or a sign. I counsel people on dreams and animal sightings and help them to understand what is being communicated. Animals often sense danger long before we do and have an uncanny ability to predict the future.

For example, I remember driving into Yellowstone National Park and all the animals were running and flying together out of the park, just like a Disney movie. Deer were running next to wolves, hawks were flying alongside owls, it seemed like all of life in the park went past my car in the opposite direction as I drove in through the gate. I stopped and asked a ranger what on earth was going on. He told me a fire had started some distance away and he pointed to a ridge far off in the distance. The smoke was not yet visible to the human eye. But the animals knew.

Some people have a similar ability – precognition; the ability to see the future. Whether we like it or not we are often fearful of what is to come and prefer a fixed routine that allows for little surprise and change. In ancient times humans would look to the demi gods for predictions about the future. The local medicine man or woman was trusted by the deities with the guidance not only for the people but with what was to come in the future. Today, we put a lot of trust in data and technology for future predictions but despite our reliance on science, often times, it is still our hunches, our mass intuitive feelings that governs us – you only have to take a look at the stock market for proof.

Above all, humans are guided by their emotional intelligence and at the center is the heart and a force more powerful than life itself, love. Its power is so immense and transformative it can take us beyond duality. Even though all the stories in *Dancing with Raven and Bear* are original they honor the message of my ancestors – love everyone at the deepest level of your being. In all of my years of healing people, pets, and spirits I have found that our greatest power is love and that is reflected in many of the stories here. Through love we can ignite a level of freedom we might have never known.

Freedom is found in the little things we feel and do like getting off work early and going to the park. Skipping school or finding ten minutes that just belong to you. Our freedom is up to us and provides a pathway that connects our hearts to Creator and the Earth. May you live your life like a tree reaching for the stars and grounding deep into the Earth. May your experience be one of Earth Medicine that you can walk with each step holding awareness, consciousness and healing within. May you connect deeply with this planet and receive the many gifts she shares that remain in the unseen world but are felt in the heart and soul of humanity.

About the Author

Photo by Danielle Richardson

Sonja Grace is an internationally known mystic and healer, whose work helps people who suffer physically, mentally, emotionally, and spiritually. She is an energy surgeon who defies time and space with her ability to spirit travel to work with her clients wherever they are in the world; she performs all levels of healing, including restructuring tissue and repairing organs, bones, blood, and cells. Sonja's ancestral background is a fascinating blend of Native American and Norwegian. Adopted by Hopis on the reservation in Arizona, Sonja is considered a medicine woman.

Sonja is the author of *Become an Earth Angel* and *Spirit Traveler: Unlocking Ancient Mysteries and Secrets of Eight of the World's Great Historic Sites*. She lives in Arizona, USA. For information on Sonja's workshops, retreats, and more, visit her website: **https://sonjagrace.com**.

FINDHORN PRESS

Life-Changing Books

Learn more about us and our books at
www.findhornpress.com

For information on the Findhorn Foundation:
www.findhorn.org